BY SLOANE CROSLEY

FICTION

The Clasp

NONFICTION

Look Alive Out There
How Did You Get This Number
I Was Told There'd Be Cake

Look
Alive
Out
There

SLOANE CROSLEY

Look
Alive
Out
There

ESSAYS

MCD ⊛ FARRAR, STRAUS AND GIROUX   NEW YORK

MCD

Farrar, Straus and Giroux

175 Varick Street, New York 10014

These essays originally appeared, in somewhat different form, in the following publications: "A Dog Named Humphrey" in *The Believer*; "Up the Down Volcano" as an e-book; "Immediate Family" in *The New York Times*. "A Dog Named Humphrey" was published when *Gossip Girl* was still on the air. May she rest in peace. xoxo

Library of Congress Cataloging-in-Publication Data

Names: Crosley, Sloane, author.

Title: Look alive out there : essays / Sloane Crosley.

Description: First edition. | New York : MCD / Farrar, Straus and Giroux, 2018.

Identifiers: LCCN 2017038323 | ISBN 9780374279844 (hardcover) |

ISBN 9780374711801 (ebook)

Classification: LCC PS3603.R673 A6 2018 | DDC 814/.6—dc23

LC record available at https://lccn.loc.gov/2017038323

Designed by Abby Kagan

Our books may be purchased in bulk for promotional, educational, or business use. Please contact your local bookseller or the Macmillan Corporate and Premium Sales Department at 1-800-221-7945, extension 5442, or by e-mail at MacmillanSpecialMarkets@macmillan.com.

www.mcdbooks.com • www.fsgbooks.com

Follow us on Twitter, Facebook, and Instagram at @mcdbooks

1 3 5 7 9 10 8 6 4 2

This is a work of nonfiction. However, the names and identifying characteristics of certain individuals have been changed, some timelines have been altered, and some of the dialogue is more exact than some of the other dialogue.

To Russell Perreault. Thank God you're so pretty.

When you live past the age of rebellion, and you still rebel,
you seem to yourself a kind of senile Lucifer.

— E. M. CIORAN

Contents

Look
Alive
Out
There

Wheels
Up

I AM RUNNING LATE FOR THE AIRPORT, TRYING TO CATCH A CAB ON
my street corner. A woman in a wheelchair and her date, a man,
arrive at the corner seconds after me. They pretend not to see
me and I pretend not to see them, which is the kind of cutthroat
strategy New Yorkers employ when embarking on otherwise benign activities. It's partially to avoid conflict and partially to claim
innocence in the event of the finger. As the minutes pass and no
cabs come, the tension grows. I make a big show of checking the
time and rotating my suitcase back and forth. At long last, a cab
drifts in our direction. Under normal circumstances the cab would
be mine. I have the clear lead. But this particular vehicle is the

model with the sliding doors, designated for handicapped access. Seeing as how my plane will definitely crash if I steal a cab from a woman in a wheelchair, I step aside.

"Here," I say, "you guys take it."

"Thanks so much," says the man.

And for a whole three seconds, everyone in this scenario feels very good about themselves. The lack of fanfare is a kind of fanfare in itself, a celebration that society has not yet broken down into breadlines and ATM-based riots. We do not throw our handicapped under the bus. We move to the back of the bus for them.

The cab door gapes open on its tracks. The man leans down and puts a hand on each armrest of the wheelchair. He kisses the woman sweetly in what I assume is a casual assertion of their love. Then he unhands the chair and springs into the cab by himself. He waves at her from the open window. The cab wheels off in one direction, the woman in the other.

One of the very few things of which I am certain is that it's not possible to be handicapped by association. Being in the social orbit of a person in a wheelchair does not entitle you to special accommodations and it certainly does not entitle you to someone else's cab. In a huff, I tug my luggage to the next block, thinking about how this man is the worst person to have ever lived. Meanwhile, the woman is just ahead of me. I begin to judge her, too. Physical impediments are nontransferable, but social ones are. You are who you kiss goodbye.

We stay the course for a couple of blocks. She's covering twice as much ground. It's unclear if she's fleeing the scene or just more adept at slicing through crowds. But I try to catch up with her. Should an available cab arrive, I plan on announcing my urgent destination to the driver so that *certain* people might feel very guilty indeed.

We pass a liquor store where someone has tied up a dog outside. The dog, a bright-eyed mutt, sits with his legs stretched out on the pavement. Without so much as a swerve, the woman wheels over his tail. The dog jumps up and lets out a high-pitched yelp. The woman keeps going. Bystanders are transformed into witnesses. Upon hearing his pet's cry, the dog's owner comes charging out of the store, looking for answers. The store's cashier stands in the doorway. Everyone hesitates to finger the culprit.

"That woman," I say, pointing. "She wheeled over his tail."

The man's face morphs from enraged to sympathetic as he registers this lady, forever seated, waiting for a traffic light to change.

"Oh," he says, backing down, "she probably didn't realize."

The dog, by now, has recovered from the incident. But I have not.

"No," I correct him, "she realized—she just didn't care."

The man shrugs. The dog plows his wet nose into his owner's palm. The whole point of pets is to have a living annex of your personality filled with all the qualities you'd like to have but don't. Instant forgiveness is one of those qualities. If this guy is going to be so magnanimous, it seems redundant that he should even have a dog.

"She's in a *wheelchair*," the cashier pipes up behind me. "What's the matter with you?"

Outside
Voices

WE HAD A TOWNHOUSE BUT WE WEREN'T ALLOWED TO TOUCH IT.
I had to be lifted up by the armpits to peer inside. The brick façade
appeared to be cut from a single sheet, but if you looked closely,
you could see how my father had smeared cement onto miniature
bricks with a butter knife. The townhouse was electric, too, mod-
eled after its 1920s counterpart and outfitted with stained-glass
lamps and micro-editions of *Moby-Dick* and *Jane Eyre*. There were
even lights on the outside, brass sconces that framed the doorway
and cast shadows on the perennially green hedges below.

The house I grew up in is not like this. It's compact and boxy,
built on a cement slab and encased in vinyl siding. On the Tim

Burton Sliding Architectural Scale, it's less *Beetlejuice,* more *Edward Scissorhands.* Ours is one of two models of homes on the street. It's as if an architect approached the neighborhood the way you approach a child at mealtime. You're not supposed to ask a child to conjure an ideal dinner out of thin air; you're supposed to say "Chicken or spaghetti?" or all hell breaks loose. The neighborhood itself is shaped like a ladle with four lines of streets cutting across the middle and one long one, which bends before merging into some woods. My parents live in the soup, surrounded by neighbors making an effort with koi ponds.

My whole life, my parents refused to do the decent thing and pretend they couldn't hear every step I took. I have never been trapped in a bunker or a submarine, but I have to assume there's an understanding in these situations. These people would never survive. If I picked up the phone in the kitchen, my father's voice would come booming from the basement, asking who I was calling. If I unfolded a blanket in the den, my mother would shout down from the top floor, offering me another one. If I passed their bedroom door, they would demand to know what I was up to. Seems harmless enough until you know that the only room after theirs was the bathroom.

Thus, the townhouse became my platonic ideal of a house. It was always grand and peaceful. It stood in the corner of the living room, covered with a tarp like a birdcage. Light from the television would be visible to any tiny people living inside. They would be able to hear my parents' cries of "What are you watching?" as I changed the channel. But there were no tiny people beneath the tarp. No eyes to see or ears to hear. No one to tell me that I would one day live in Manhattan, where if someone follows you around, asking you who you're calling, you can have that person arrested.

* * *

A couple of decades later I was living in a railroad apartment in Chelsea, illegally subletting it from a friend's sister. The sister lived in Los Angeles and I never met her, despite repeated offers to meet whenever I happened to be in Los Angeles. This was for her benefit, not mine. If it were me, I'd want to vet me. But I never heard back from her. I never heard from her at all, actually. One time the peephole fell out, a thing I did not realize peepholes could do—just dislodge themselves and come thudding onto the floor like a car part. I wrote to her, explaining what had happened. No response. Eventually, I taped the receipt for a new peephole to my reduced rent check, which she cashed without a, well—you know. The second I saw her name appear on my phone, I knew I was getting evicted.

Not wanting to stray too far from home, I paid a broker to find me a place nearby. In the easiest gig of that guy's already unchallenging career, we walked nine blocks south to a prewar building, the kind with a name engraved above the awning but none of the residents could tell you what it is. The broker unlocked the door to a 600-square-foot one-bedroom on the second floor that had been recently occupied by a boy (the clothes pole in the closet was missing). But the moldings were thick enough to double as bookshelves and the view was unreal. Dogwood trees shaded a row of the private backyards of townhouses. Cherry blossom detritus drizzled in the wind. A blue jay landed on the fire escape.

It was the first apartment I saw, I could barely afford it, and I took it immediately.

The West Village is a ridiculous place to call home. People with unseemly bank accounts spend thousands of dollars freshening the flowerpots on their stoops. Rosebushes, hydrangeas, pansies, and zinnias—all casually exposed to marauding vagrants. Except there are no vagrants, not even marauding ones. It's a generationally diverse area but otherwise it's as removed from reality as a movie set. Celebrities' kids skip along the pavement, backpacks twice their size bobbing up and down. One of the houses visible from my apartment is owned by an elderly couple. The woman likes to tell guests how Hilary Swank used to climb a fence and exit through their house in order to avoid the paparazzi.

Down the block and around the clock, people take photos of the façade of Carrie Bradshaw's apartment in *Sex and the City*. Submitting to their fate, the real owners have installed a donation box on behalf of a local animal shelter for every photo taken. These tourists' heads would explode like a bomb full of nicotine patches if they knew that Sarah Jessica Parker herself lives around the corner. I can't help but wonder what she feels when she walks past Carrie's building. It must be like driving past your high school, at once everything and nothing.

I only cared about the celebrities the way all New Yorkers care about celebrities: I ignored them or, if they were especially famous, congratulated myself for ignoring them. The real draw of the neighborhood was the quiet. And not just any kind of quiet. Here, in the heart of Manhattan, was a pod of that suburban silence that had eluded me as a child. You could hear a pin drop in my bedroom—on the bed. Early mornings, I listened to the heckling of seagulls that had strayed inland from the Hudson River. On warm evenings, a cellist sat on the street corner with his case open. When it rained, water pelted the leaves outside my enchanted tree house.

* * *

And then one day the leaves dropped and Jared came out. Jared lived in the townhouse directly behind my apartment. He must have been on summer vacation or touring Europe by colonial rickshaw when I moved in. Jared was between fifteen and eighteen years of age. It was impossible to tell. I could never get a good read on his height, as his resting state was slouched in a lawn chair, watching viral videos on his phone at full volume. And I never heard him say stuff like "Looks like I can be legally tried as an adult now," despite being someone for whom the distinction was clearly relevant.

How do I begin to explain my relationship with this creature? Is it a relationship if you've never met? Certainly this is an acceptable dynamic online, but played out in real life it's called stalking. All five of the windows in my apartment faced Jared's house. And for as many years, I heard every word this kid said. I would like to tell you that his woes were typical of his age bracket: unrequited crushes, parental oppression, social strife. But Jared had no woes. Plato advised us to be kind, everyone you meet is fighting a hard battle, but I am here to tell you that I have witnessed Plato's exception. Jared's battles centered around selecting the right surfboard (for show or for use at a beach house, both equally abhorrent) and the occasional obligation to come inside and set the table. And that he didn't *have* to do, so long as he ignored the sound of his own name. Jewish guilt is no match for teenage entitlement.

I rarely saw the father, who was probably off somewhere, devaluing my 401(k). The little sister was shy and kept to herself. The mother was an upscale fashion photographer. She had a Susan Sontag streak in her hair and doled out advice like "Don't do anything I wouldn't do." Occasionally, she would pace in the backyard, phone in hand, all puffed up about some dead-eyed model. But for the most part, the yard was Jared's domain—a place to smoke cigarettes, molest a guitar, and throw raging parties.

Lest you think I don't know what I signed up for by living on the most densely populated slip of land in America, rest assured that I do. There are sounds one learns to accept, even to be lulled by on occasion. Jackhammers that emerge seasonally and peck at the concrete like oversized woodpeckers. Screaming matches that make you grateful you're not one of the two people in that relationship. I have lived over DJs, newborn babies, sheet-metal sculptors, and Ping-Pong patios. In Chelsea, I lived above a piano player, who practiced scales. When I could stand it no longer, I sheepishly knocked on his door. He apologized and vowed never to practice scales in the house again. Which is how I wound up listening to "I'm a Yankee Doodle Dandy" every day for a year.

But Jared's noise was different. It did not disrupt me, because disruption implies separation of activity, the intervening of outside elements. Rather, Jared's world became my world. I was paying rent like a single person but living with an entire family in what amounted to an inaccessible wing of my apartment. Every afternoon, Jared and his friends returned home from whatever educational womb they attended and clunked down the backyard steps, blaring music and demonstrating familiarity with one another's last names. Jared was quick to laugh, which would have been his best quality were it not for the laugh's resemblance to a hyena being choked to death by bubble wrap. His cackle was like one of those purposefully ugly sculptures, the kind of art that considers your irritation an accomplishment. Really, I can't say enough bad things about it.

They say smell is the strongest trigger of memory, but let us not underestimate the bone-chilling power of sound. The sound of cigarettes being packed against a table. The sound of tracks being skipped. The sound of a porch door banging. These were the harbingers, the sounds of my torturers clearing their throats. Sometimes Jared would leave the music on after he left, a tactic generally employed by war criminals. But mostly he and his friends stayed put, multiplying like gremlins.

Does it seem like I was spying? I was and I wasn't. This was not so much a *Rear Window* situation as it was a window situation. If I was home, I was on an involuntary stakeout. If I was out, some perverse part of me hoped they would be in the yard when I returned, because then I could stop worrying about them being in the yard. Anthropologically, I was fascinated. Never in my life have I had a social circle as wide or as regular as Jared's. Then again, I have also never lived in a five-story townhouse. It's hard to say how much the house itself factored into Jared's popularity. Surely his cohorts—preppy boys with laughs that died in their throats and coltish girls with sea-level self-esteem—slumbered in comparable accommodations.

Very occasionally it was just Jared, alone in the backyard,

pouring out the decibels. The mother would appear at the top of the stairs, mumbling something about homework. And he'd tell her to fuck off, which she fully deserved. Jared was a menace, true, but who had let him get that way? I remember with a haunting clarity lying in bed one night, being kept conscious by Biggie Smalls, when the mother screamed Jared's name. My heart fluttered. Finally. An adult. An authority figure. A savior with her finger on the allowance button.

"Jared!" she shrieked. "Where'd you put the corkscrew?"

* * *

Of course I did. Of course I asked them to be quiet. *Hey guys, sorry to be a buzzkill, but can you keep it down? Hey guys, can you take it inside your mansion because I have nowhere to run?* To which they apologized in a tone that suggested "sorry" was more of a password than a feeling. So I bought a white-noise machine and fancy headphones. I slept on my side to deafen one chosen ear. None of it worked. Finally, I bit the bullet and called 311, a placebo service for cranks on the brink. Operators forward complaints to local police precincts, at which point the police have eight hours to take action, assuming they're done mocking you. Also: an eight-hour window? Even Jared didn't party from midnight until 8 a.m. He lived in a townhouse, not a warehouse.

I pretended to write down my service request number because, for some reason, it's impossible to admit you don't want your service request number. Alas, help was never sent—a bad sign for me, a worse one for my fellow citizens who actually needed it.

I resented Jared for turning me into a curmudgeon before my

time. I was not old enough to be so angry, to delude myself into thinking I would be the one to teach these pesky kids a lesson. But the feeling of powerlessness was all-consuming. They were like cicadas without the bonus years of dormancy. The whole family worked in shifts. Between 7 and 8 a.m., their yapping terrier was released so that it could give every stick of lawn furniture a piece of its mind. Before noon, a housekeeper came to collect the previous night's beer bottles, tossing them in a garbage bag. Then Jared and his friends would emerge, well rested, recapping the night while the sister sat worshipfully at their feet. Later that afternoon, she practiced her dance routines. I couldn't beat them.

One day, I decided to cut out the middleman. I marched into the local police station myself. I made an errand out of it: Grocery shopping, check. Laundry, check. Quick narc run, check. A sympathetic cop scribbled her direct extension on the back of a blank parking ticket. It felt electric in my hand. When Jared threw a party the next night, I unfolded the ticket.

"They might be the worst people of their generation," I told her, gilding the pity lily.

After a mere hour, I peered out the window to see the cop standing in Jared's doorway. The floor-to-ceiling windows on both sides of the house meant that I could see straight through it, to the glossy doors of more townhouses. Jared, stripped of his bravado by a woman in uniform, slumped his shoulders and shut the door. The music stopped. The chatter ceased. I flipped my pillow to the cooler side.

I woke several hours later to the choral opening of "You Can't Always Get What You Want." My subconscious had tried to incorporate this second wave of the party into my dreams. But my subconscious had done all it could. It was time to deliver me unto reality.

* * *

Weeks turned into months. I started keeping a notebook by my bed:

> *Jared spits grapes into the air and tries to catch them in his mouth.*
> *Jared feels like he's seen some pictures of your dick from the 8th grade.*
> *Jared has decided tequila gives you diarrhea.*
> *Jared thinks this is some Cheech and Chong shit.*
> *Jared has discovered jazz.*

By documenting his activities, I thought perhaps I could trick myself into thinking I had signed up for this. Like a scientist observing a nocturnal creature. Or I'd try to offset the hot rage coursing through my veins by envisioning scenarios in which Jared's existence served to bolster mine. You know what I need? I need to Windex every surface of my apartment at 4 a.m. Thanks, Jared, for saving me the trouble of setting an alarm or buying drugs of my own.

The woman who lived in the apartment next to mine did not have the box seats I did, but she did have a four-month-old baby. I asked her if the people in the back ever bothered her.

"Oh, you mean Jared?" she groaned. "When we moved in, he

was still a little kid. I thought he was so cute, playing in the back-yard. But you know what they say about tiger cubs."

"What do they say?"

"Don't adopt tiger cubs."

I felt the pulse of their lives steadily behind me. Not just phys-ically behind me, but in time. I was watching them go through their formative years (some had lost their virginity, some were just pretending). I was waiting for them to grow up, desperate for the glue to set, for the clay to dry, for the inexorable metamorphosis that would bring about their conscious selves. But I couldn't keep waiting without getting older myself. Their very existence high-lighted my own aging in a way that jarred me. Before Jared, only events in my own life—a friend's marriage, a sick parent, the twen-tieth anniversary of a seminal movie—had triggered ruminations on the passage of time. Which meant that, despite the stresses of aging, I had always had a manageable view of it. I reflected at will. But after Jared, my own mortality could smack me in the face at random. If I was in a good mood when I heard him, I found myself eager to learn something from his youth and to be reminded of my own. If I was in a bad mood, I never wanted to hear from a person so much as a day younger than me so long as I lived.

They say holding on to resentment is like letting someone take up space in your brain rent-free, and my rent was pretty high as it was. But I couldn't help it. I talked about Jared to strangers, to editors, to physicians, to hairdressers and bus drivers. Okay, one bus driver. But I think we can all agree that's one too many. I talked about Jared with people I admired—people who I meant to tell how much I loved their work but all that came out was Jared vomit. I talked about him at book fairs, in towns and cities across the land. I went on CBS *This Morning* to discuss an op-ed I had written but Jared had kept me up the night before, teaching himself to play "Go On with Your Bad Self" on the guitar. So I talked about him with Charlie Rose.

Out of helpfulness or exasperation, friends floated suggestions.

"Why don't you—"

"Shoot them?" I interrupted. "I can't shoot them."

"—move out."

It hadn't occurred to me. Rather, it had occurred to me that murder was more of an option than moving. A true test of a New Yorker if there ever was one. I was fully aware there were other apartments I could live in, other boroughs I could go to. But to live in New York is to weigh your traumas, and moving is a formidable one. Plus, while I might not have been here first, I was here truest. I respected my apartment. I did not litter it with beer cans and try to set the furniture on fire. Instead, I begged for mercy. *Please be quiet. Please please please.* I did this sparingly, concerned about its diminishing effects but mostly concerned about something utterly mortifying: Jared's impression of me.

Jared was cool. He just was. What's worse, he plugged into some residual teenage part of me that wanted to be cool, too. At first I dismissed him as "high school cool." Naturally other teenagers laughed at his lewd jokes—their bars were just as low. But signs of Jared's enduring cool were emerging. For starters, the kid had great taste in music. You know what they say: If I can Shazam you, you're too close. Yet even as I wanted to destroy him, I would nonchalantly reach my phone into the air. The Velvet Underground. Nina Simone. The Black Angels. Townes van Zandt. Charlotte Gainsbourg (who lived across the street). He had access to every hot spot in the city and would make plans to patronize places I had only seen in passing. Meanwhile, he started to diversify his friends. The milquetoast-looking blonds in Irish fisherman sweaters still appeared, but so did black guys with white sneakers, Hispanic girls with red sneakers, and one guy with a Mohawk. They were like the American dream come to life, friends united by a force stronger than acceptance—money. And their banter improved. They had heated political debates. The girls doted on the younger sister, offering to stylize her. They teased a friend who had been in a commercial about his "bullshit acting career."

Who would they listen to now? Who could reason with them? I'd fantasize about morphing into Chris Rock or Karlie Kloss. I'll tell you what: If Karlie Kloss lifted my window wearing boy shorts and a tank top, and asked them to be quiet, they'd shut up right quick. Once, and this was a real low point, I dressed up to tell them to be quiet. I let my hair down and put on bright lipstick and a V-neck top, markers of authoritative attractiveness meant to be seen from a distance, pathetic signals that I knew from chill, that my threshold for fun was high. But by the time I opened the window, they had vanished. I leaned out into the open air. Had my dreams of their alien abduction come true? I raised my head to see the whole group had migrated to the kitchen, at least seven of them. Silhouettes of branches framed the picture. They were dancing, arms up, hips pinballing back and forth, hair swaying. Jared entered with a bag of ice, put the ice on the kitchen island, and spun one of the girls, dipping her below my sight line.

She came up, laughing. And for a full minute, I was so in love with all of them, I almost couldn't stand it.

* * *

Around this time, I began dating a younger and emotionally unavailable man who was completely wrong for me in every way but anatomically. So I fell for him. This fellow had been smacked in the face by the lucky stick, whereas I was pretty sure I felt it go whizzing past my ear once. Like Jared, he had grown up in Manhattan, though the upper part. He had Jared's surface-level deference that passed for manners, the sort of verbal salve that kept you from ever calling him an asshole because he did things like pick you up at your door. Like Jared, he was raised in a bubble of privilege. There's a bench in Central Park with his name on it, a baby gift. But unlike Jared, he had the years and the sense to try to pop the bubble with duct-tape-repaired furniture and self-funded travel to war zones. He winced at the suggestion that the universe had conspired to make his life easier, which was a huge tell— people less privileged are comfortable with acknowledging when they've had luck, because of all the times they haven't.

One evening, after I failed to properly close my bedroom blinds, Jared and his friends caught a glimpse of us naked.

"What's the relationship?" he shouted up, making a megaphone of his hands.

"You have to admit," said the emotionally unavailable man, "that's some sophisticated heckling."

Staying low, I opened the window further.

"Shut up, Jared!" I snapped.

Jared's friends snorted and slapped the table.

"Oh shit, man," said one of them, "she knows your name!"

It was the first time I'd used his name, a treat I had been saving for myself. I lay on my back and grinned at the ceiling. The emotionally unavailable man had already gotten dressed. He was paparazzi sensitive, having twice caught ex-girlfriends taking pictures of his aggressively pretty face when they thought he was asleep.

"Jared thinks the streets of London are paved with *Harry Potter* jizz," he said.

"What?" I asked, propping myself up on my elbows.

He had my notebook in his hands. I dismissed it as "notes" and he shrugged, incurious. If he had flipped the page he would have seen, written redrum-style: "Jared: why won't you graduate?" I had begun monitoring Jared's conversation for words like *application* and *early decision*. Clearly, he was old enough to have friends who had graduated. Recently, a girl had come over for dinner and Jared's mother asked how she was liking college.

"It's okay," said the girl, "I just haven't found my friend group yet."

Good, I thought. You're learning. You are not prepared for a world beyond Jared's backyard. You will inevitably seek shelter in others who are exactly like you, who know everything you know and nothing you don't, but I pray, for your sake, you never find them.

"Welp," the mother assured her. "Keep at it. You guys are our future."

That night, she hosted a birthday party for her assistant. Adult voices flooded the yard. Motown bumped against my walls.

At midnight, the wife half of the old couple leaned over their shared fence and asked the mother if she wouldn't mind keeping it down.

"It's our property, Carol," the mother shot back. "We can do what we want!"

* * *

I decided to write them a letter. I didn't write the DJ or the pianist or the newborn baby a letter. But for all my disgust, I still believed we were made of the same fundamental stuff. I had seen the mother grocery shopping and she didn't cut the line or snap at anyone. She exchanged pleasantries with the cashier and left. Be kind, I thought, for some of the people you meet are using the same organic dishwashing liquid. I believed that if they understood the impact of their actions, if they really understood, we could live in something like harmony.

I edited the letter for typos and insanity and crept around the block. I stood, looking at their gold mail slot, double-checking to be sure I hadn't flubbed the geography. The letter hated to bother them. The letter suggested that due to acoustics, it was possible that the residents of my building heard their music better than they did. An easy thing not to realize! The letter wanted to make them aware of the situation, lest they accidentally recite their bank account numbers. Ha! The letter emphasized that it had never been written before. The letter signed off on behalf of the residents of my entire building. This was quite weaselly of the letter.

I returned to my apartment just in time for Jared and his

mother to arrive home from taking the dog for a walk. What a stroke of luck, I thought, to be able to witness them open it, to see the distraught looks on their faces. The mother held a dog leash in one hand and the letter in the other. Jared read over her shoulder. Both our windows were closed, so I could not hear the peals of their laughter.

* * *

"What if he goes to NYU?" asked the emotionally unavailable man. "Or Columbia?"

We were standing at my living room window. Jared's parents had covered the yard in grass earlier that day. When Jared got home from school, he sprawled out like a Middle Eastern child who has never seen snow. A group of his peers, whom Jared referred to as "the cavalry," had come over to admire the grass.

"Maybe he won't get in," I said.

It was too horrible to contemplate. Besides, Jared never seemed to study or demonstrate flares of brilliance.

"You realize that's irrelevant."

Takes one to know one, I thought.

"Looks like fun," he said.

"No, it doesn't," I replied, even though it did, it looked very fun.

"I don't think this is going to work out," said the emotionally unavailable man, his back to the window.

He broke up with me that night, moving from emotionally unavailable to regular unavailable. Even at the height of our romance, I knew it would end like this. I could sense that I was a novelty, one of the many life experiences he was collecting en route to something else. But knowing didn't soften the blow. If anything, it made things worse. In my grief, I started hating Jared on a heretofore untold level. Jared was the raw, unadulterated version of this person who had hurt my feelings. These were people with too many escape valves built into their lives. There would always be another party, another school, another house, another country, another woman. I felt the moral responsibility of a time traveler. If I could just stop Jared from being the person he is now, I thought, he could become a better person later. Sure, he might break a heart or two, nobody's fault, but maybe he would be more torn up about it.

Armed with this larger sense of purpose, I became less preoccupied with cajoling Jared into silence. This was a good thing. But I also became vengeful, which was a bad thing. I'd figure out what song he was playing and play the same song twice as loud on a three-second delay. I'd pretend to be an emergency room doctor, lifting my window and announcing that I had to be at the hospital in two hours. They were putting other people's *lives* in danger. Once I egged his house after he went to bed. "Maturity" and "legality" were abstract notions behind my threadbare eyelids. A couple of the eggs landed on lawn chair cushions without cracking. If only I could be more like those eggs.

As Jared barreled toward graduation, he somehow got worse. The neighbors on his side of the street chimed in, their fuses growing shorter as well. The chastising was more effective coming from people who didn't have to shout from a different tax bracket. But these temporary silences could no longer satiate me. I wanted more. I wanted dark things. I wanted the parents to lose their jobs and sell the house. I wanted the kids to go to military school. I wanted to tase the dog in the throat. I wanted monsters to rise up from the earth and munch on their bones.

* * *

Jared is not keeping me from my work. Jared is my work.

* * *

Sensing I was not, in the classic sense, "hinged," my friend Charlotte attempted to cheer me up. I assured her that I was not as torn up over the emotionally unavailable man as I appeared to be. She didn't believe me. I was a wreck. Just look at me. I shouldn't lose a wink of sleep over some immature guy. She was more right than she knew.

She insisted I accompany her to an opening at an art gallery, where I didn't know many people and I didn't feel like meeting anyone. Which led me to drink. Which led me to spend a whole three minutes contemplating a sculpture that turned out to be a folding chair. Maybe I really should move, I thought. It was an emergency option, but what do you call this? My tree house had become haunted with teenage ghouls and heartache ghosts.

And that's when I saw them. Flanking the floor of the gallery was a row of massive spotlights. I approached them slowly and crouched down. Mesmerized, I touched the hot rim of one, following its path up the wall. The light stretched all the way to the ceiling.

"What are you doing?" Charlotte asked, smiling tightly at an approaching security guard.

I looked up at her, pivoting on my toes until my knees were parallel with her legs.

"Hi," I said.

"Why are you grinning like that?"

"Grinning like what?" I asked, having lost all control of my face.

* * *

Product description for 600-watt halogen light:

> This light can be set on the ground or a rooftop and aimed in the direction of the workspace. This light can also be used to powerfully illuminate a campground or construction site. Ideal for when you need to finish off a project.

"What do you have," asked the hardware store cashier, "a possum?"

I smiled and cocked my head. This was a very specific guess. But he took one look at a nonunionized woman in a sundress, sporting a canvas tote, and went straight to "possum." In return, I explained the Jared situation—the cashier threw in an on/off switch for free.

"You got an outlet by your bed?"

I nodded.

"Okay," he said, conspiratorially, "plug the extension cord into this and you plug this into the outlet and flick the switch. So you don't have to get up. You can just roll over and fuck 'em."

I never thought I would be so pleased to hear those words from a man.

I rushed home, high on revenge, exhilarated by the prospect of a new medium. Jared didn't *deserve* to hear the sound of my voice. I put one light outside on the fire escape, running the cord under my bedroom window screen, and a second one on a stool in my kitchen. Then I got into bed and waited. I checked the time. He should be home any minute now. But that night I fell asleep to the sound of the breeze rustling through the trees. Same thing happened the next night. And the next and the next. Screw you, breeze. What have you done with my juvenile delinquents?

I left town for work, planning to take the lights down when I returned. In theory, I should have been grateful. My long night of terror had ended with a whimper—but at least it had ended. That should have been good enough. But my life at that moment was populated by men who had hurt me and my vigilante streak wanted to take just one of them out. Just one.

Walking up my stairs, sifting through a week's worth of catalogs, I ran into my neighbor. Her eyes were bloodshot. Her baby was wailing.

"I might have to kill them all," she said, her voice cracking.

"He's back?" I asked, trying to temper my glee.

"No," she said, "not him . . . her."

* * *

My dreams of Jared going off to college had, unceremoniously, come to pass. Or perhaps there had been a ceremony. Perhaps a graduation rager had taken place and I hadn't been home for it. It didn't matter. The sister had ascended the throne of torment with gusto. Years of watching Jared and his friends had taught her everything she needed to know. The sister's friends—younger, wilder, louder—made Jared's look like a prayer circle. They had inherited Jared's playlist but beyond that, it was just a sea of ill-formed estrogen. The sister's cavalry was into shit like daring one another to throw bottles against the house and setting off fireworks. Clumps of girls spread out on the grass, taking selfies, contemplating future tattoos, failing to have seen the movie *Thirteen*.

"For Valentine's Day, my mom got my dad strippers," the sister bragged. "They did flaming shots out of their assholes and now my mom is, like, best friends with the strippers."

I closed my eyes and felt the corners of my lips curl. I washed my face and brushed my teeth. I flossed. Then I got into bed, rolled over, and fucked 'em.

Their yard lit up as if a helicopter were preparing to land on it.

"What the hell?!" they cried, confused and squinting.

"Turn that off!" they cried.

"That's annoying us!" they cried.

One of them called me a cunt, which I did not think they had in them. It takes a certain kind of girl to bypass "bitch." Because they were animals, they threw rocks, and because they were drunk, they missed. The sister tried to reclaim her authority by deploying the only logic in her arsenal.

"It's our property!" she shouted. "We can do what we want!"

I yawned. In the months to come, I would reward good be-havior with darkness, but that night I left the lights on, even after they admitted defeat and went inside.

There was a pleasant, almost celestial glow that illuminated my apartment. This was the light bouncing off their windows and into mine. I thought of the evening I saw Jared and his friends dancing in their kitchen, of how gorgeously happy they all looked. I tried mustering some of that old generosity of spirit, but whatever heartstrings had tied my world to theirs had gone slack. Ques-tions drifted through my fading consciousness: Would the sister call her brother at college and tell him about this? Would he be impressed by the enemy's tactics? And, really, who cared? I couldn't be bothered to worry about what people like that thought of me anymore. Their lives were out there and mine was in here. They were forever behind me in time, as unable to catch up as I was to wait for them. All around me, the shadows of tree branches stretched across the walls—branches that lived only because they were connected to a trunk in Jared's yard.

A
Dog
Named
Humphrey

WHEN THE OPPORTUNITY TO APPEAR ON THE TEEN DRAMA *GOSSIP Girl* came my way, I felt like I had won a contest. Not a contest it would have occurred to me to enter, but the type of contest of which I am dimly aware as a result of living in the world. Instead of cars or cash, the prize is people. Yes, people. Be pulled onstage by Bono and have him lick your face! Have a very light lunch with Kate Moss! Some philosophical confusions arise—for both the winner and the prize—when it comes to packaging real people and presenting them as if they were objects to be bid upon and bartered, as if their allotted hours on Earth were more valuable than yours.

For one thing, it strikes me as vaguely denigrating to the celebrities. And I say this as someone not historically concerned with the denigration of celebrities. But the underlying message to civilians seems to be that a celebrity life is best accessed not through hard work or talent but through lottery-type luck. Their fortune is a fluke that, with a flick of the wrist, could belong to any man on the street. What a lesson. And what of us civilian participants? Are we not setting ourselves up to feel bad about our modest level of notoriety, a level with which we were perfectly comfortable just the day before? Then there's the shame of the thrill, the tiny hope that someone famous will whip around and call you a natural, tell you they see the faint outline of your high school production of *Pippin* in your delivery. Is it healthy to place this much value on the celebrity gaze? We are, at best, pleased by the scraps. We are, at worst, validated by them.

These were the kinds of thoughts swirling around my head after I got the call. The prize I'd won—the chance to mingle, and for a moment be an equal, with the actors on the set of *Gossip Girl*—was not initially meant to be mine. Hollywood is not known for its sensitivity; I was told outright that a more famous writer had been offered the walk-on and declined. The news that someone I respected would not do what I was willing to do in a heartbeat had absolutely no effect on me. I did not slavishly follow *Gossip Girl*, but I certainly knew what it was. I was familiar with the premise, knew what channel it was on, and had watched parts of the first season. The show is what my grandmother used to call "good junk" because she died before the phrase "guilty pleasure" entered the lexicon. Because I was tickled by the invitation, I told myself that the famous author had clearly said no because she was unfamiliar with the show's good-junkiness—not because she was weighing the benefits of playing a caricature of a writer and making her decision based on what a serious author should or should not do.

But when I hung up the phone, I thought: Which is what, exactly?

* * *

What's unclear to me, even now, is how I missed the part where I would be playing myself. I knew I wasn't being solicited for my acting skills. But I thought I'd just be a mute extra, waving stiffly while someone pulled my skateboard in slow motion across the background.

I learned otherwise when the script was e-mailed to me the night before. The episode is called "Memoirs of an Invisible Dan" and the scene is a book party thrown in honor of the book's author, Dan Humphrey, the scruffy Brooklyn-based progeny of a former rock star and, as such, a distastefully pedigreed outsider to the Upper East Side world of *Gossip Girl*. Dan, because he attended an exclusive high school and dated one of its queen bees, has snuck an insider peek (thus the title of his book, meant ironically: *Insider*) at a life he is doomed to distantly watch. This condemnation becomes increasingly hard to swallow as the series unfolds, given Dan's social, carnal, and claustrophobically familial connections to this cloistered world. His father marries his girlfriend's mother. None of these ties deters him from jotting down his spiky observations. And observe he has done. After scoring a short-story publication in *The New Yorker* as a high school junior (a "dream on" incident of implausibility that's become increasingly plausible in these days' youth-prized scribes), Dan, in true Truman Capote fashion, writes a roman à clef about his tony friends and the socially stratospheric family into which his father has married. He is then embarrassed by the publication because he fears they will confuse fact and fiction, as they definitely should.

Which is where I come in. In my scene, a snappily dressed young woman playing a literary agent escorts me to a group of actors. These include Dan's father and stepmother (Rufus Humphrey and Lily van der Woodsen, played by Matthew Settle and Kelly Rutherford) and their stepson, a dastardly but lovable peer of Dan's (Chuck Bass, played by Ed Westwick). Chuck is the motherless son of a ruthless business scion; his broody eyebrow acting is a triumph. *Gossip Girl* is not so much about teenagers with grown-up problems as it is about New Yorkers with Dallas problems.

According to the script, I am to be presented in a manner reminiscent of *Wikipedia: The Movie*—

"And this is Sloane Crosley," says the literary agent.

She is instructed to step aside and gesture at me before helpfully adding, "The bestselling author of *I Was Told There'd Be Cake*."

Then the whole group is meant to *ooh* and *ahh* as if I had invented the cheese grater.

As one of the many people who go through life not being Bono, I was grateful for the plug. I just didn't want to be standing right there, the camera zooming in on my face as I watched the plug enter the outlet. At a real book party, such information would be encased in a quiet murmuring and the subject would be far across the room. If at all. Talking about an author's book at a book party isn't quite as gauche as talking about an artist's painting at a gallery opening, but it's up there. What people really talk about at book parties is a mixture of small talk and smack talk, making the occasional meal out of whatever morsel of scandal has fallen into their laps. They drink free wine and look for warm bodies with which to flirt. In other words: *Gossip Girl* without the plot.

Perhaps if I were playing a version of myself instead of myself, I would have had less of a flushed reaction to the line. I was conversant enough in the show to know that a decent number of New Yorkers had made cameos on *Gossip Girl*, among them Cynthia Rowley, Michael Bloomberg, and Lisa Loeb. A motley but expensively shampooed crew. This roster of past guest stars is part of the reason I was excited. *Gossip Girl* has been unusually good to Manhattan-based people and industries via name drops, guest appearances, and product placements. Being invited into this world (even as a backup choice) felt like a minor local knighting conducted on national television.

More than that, a surprising number of book-publishing figures and authors have appeared on *Gossip Girl*. Further reconnaissance taught me that over the course of several seasons, Jay McInerney plays a once-young-'n'-famous writer named Jeremiah Harris. Jeremiah gives advice to young Dan, then interning at a Condé Nast publication and struggling to become young-'n'-famous, too. Jonathan Karp, an editor and publisher at Simon & Schuster, appears several times on the show because S&S is publishing *Insider* whether Dan is ready for it or not, goddamn it; Blair, another private school queen bee, is close personal friends with Lorrie Moore and invites her to a party; Jeffrey Eugenides and Jennifer Egan get shout-outs; editors at *The Paris Review* are clamoring to get a look at Dan's prose.

The thing is, all these people's roles are proportional to their relevance to the *Gossip Girl* world. If they are recurring and substantive enough, they have separate character names. When Wallace Shawn plays Cyrus Rose and dates Blair's mother, it's difficult to get past his Wallace Shawn–ness, but, in a way, we're not meant to. Normally we judge an actor by how quickly that actor can make us forget reality. However, the *Gossip Girl* producers know a significant swath of their fan base will recognize Wallace Shawn and Jay McInerney on sight. So why bother with forgetting when we can appreciate the clever meta-ness of the show's writers and experience pride at our own cleverness for getting the reference?

Whether you're playing yourself or a wink-wink persona, the law of cameo syllogism goes as follows (stay with me, here): If you spend a certain amount of screen time playing yourself, you are no longer yourself but a version of yourself—a stereotype of you. Add a bonus layer of confusion if you are playing a stereotype of you in a scene in which all the characters are outraged by the possibility that the fictional characters in a fictional book published by a real publishing house might be based on the real fictional selves they're playing.

What falls off the conveyor belt? Sloane is the bestselling author of *I Was Told There'd Be Cake*.

Prior to becoming a full-time writer, I worked for many years as a book publicist. As someone who used to cart around awkward literary geniuses for a living, I tried to imagine a scenario in which introducing an author as "bestselling" wouldn't go off like a bomb. Deep down, I knew the *Gossip Girl* writers were doing me a favor. They were trying to introduce me to the people *watching* the party, not *at* the party. As we'll surely recall, I was no one's first choice. But my appreciation for this kindness was diminished by my next line: "Which I am still in search of."

Here I am referring to actual cake. This syntax is complicated and awkwardly phrased, and sounds like I'm contorting myself to express a desire in a grammatically correct fashion, even if the result is not grammatically correct. *Which I am still in search of.* It's not dissimilar to the reality-TV-show contestant's ungrammatical attempt to appear grammatical, a quirk of using the subject pronoun after a preposition, instead of the correct object version. So: You have to choose between Brad or I.

In terms of verisimilitude, however, the line rings true. *Which I am still in search of.* It sounds like I am saying whatever gobble-dygook is required to get me out of a conversation at a party. It's called method acting.

My next line after that: "So if you'll excuse me . . ."

I trail off. So preoccupied is this me-version character by the possibility of stuffing her face with cake, she has no mind for small talk.

"Oh, it is so nice to meet you!" exclaims an impressed Lily van der Woodsen.

And then?

Then nothing.

That's it.

I don't have another line.

I look Lily dead in the eye, ignore Dan's father, Rufus Humphrey, and Rufus and Lily's stepson, Chuck, and scurry away. Rufus opens his mouth and looks as if he's about to add a pleasantry of his own. Alas, I have already turned my back to him.

The writers of the episode surely did not realize how strangely this would translate once the cameras were rolling. Or, more likely, they didn't think twice about it, because it's an expendable moment of civilian bumbling during a show that's been on the air for years. I am left holding the bad-manners bag. But I am also a guest in the house of *Gossip Girl*, afraid to ad-lib. I am convinced it's on the same spectrum as inquiring about my "motivation." So I stick to the script and say nothing more.

I hear Lily's words as I flee the scene.

"Oh, it is so nice to meet you!"

You bet your ass it was.

*   *   *

Gossip Girl calls the Upper East Side home, but the day of my appearance, it was being filmed on the Upper West Side; a minor park-width fudge considering all of the far-flung locales Vancouver claims to be. I didn't care where I was going, so long as I would be lent something to wear. This was the first prediction my girlfriends made, offering an "I bet they'll dress you!" if they were fans of the show and an "At least they'll dress you" if they weren't. The *Gossip Girl* wardrobe is one of its more preposterous elements but one I could really get behind. Movies and television shows set in New York have a reputation for being visually unrealistic, and they can get away with it because the idea of New York held by real people is so unrealistic. And I'm not talking about someone in a midwestern town watching syndicated episodes of *Friends*. I'm talking about the people who actually live here.

The city is big and varied enough that it's always possible that someone out there is leading the life portrayed on-screen. There could very well be teenagers akin to the ones on *Gossip Girl*, living on their own in the Waldorf Astoria, wearing berets en route to drug deals, sending back plates of spaghetti Bolognese at the Bowery. You may not know them personally. But they're out there, leading pretty much your same life—just with a few more rhinestones glued to the edges. I've seen glimpses of them, or the people I think might be them, at literary benefits that I have rarely paid for when I was acting as escort to other authors, keeping folded copies of their tour schedules in my bag.

These events notwithstanding, book publicity is an unglamorous job. In my time working in publishing, I never once dressed up for a book party. Wearing a nice dress at a book function generally indicates that you are fresh from (a) a job interview, (b) a funeral, or (c) a fake funeral to cover up the interview you just came from. For the handful of fancy events the publishing industry hosts each year, I would bring a change of clothing with me to the office and hop into a dress in the handicapped bathroom stall. But even these occasions were increasingly rare. Cocktails had been replaced by beer, restaurants by dive bars, gift bags by the code for the bathroom door. The big book-launch party itself had become unrealistic, even in reality.

Thus when the *Gossip Girl* producers encouraged me to bring what I might wear to "a typical fictional publishing cocktail party," I was disappointed. Yes, I was playing me, but did I have to dress like it? Also, I had never attended a typical fictional publishing cocktail party before. I don't own any hypothetical dresses.

* * *

Gossip Girl is taped many months before it airs, so the pressure is on not only to wear something chic, but to wear something that will remain chic in the future. With no time to shop, I threw a few hardly stained dresses into a plastic garment bag and made my way out into the rain. It was pouring by the time I arrived uptown. I met a production assistant outside the apartment building, hangers cutting off my thumb circulation, and exchanged my small umbrella for her large one. She escorted me to a silver trailer and knocked on the door, whereupon two stylists yanked me inside as if I were a spy about to blow my cover.

Maybe the inside of the *Gossip Girl* wardrobe trailer is normal. Maybe it's not objectively impressive if you work in television. But I had never seen anything like it. It had sliding ladders and tiers of clothing racks. The names of the characters were taped to various wooden drawers and they said things like BLAIR: TIGHTS, STRAPLESS BRAS. I wondered if we were the same size and if I could be the kind of person who steals a bra as a souvenir. I did come here to act. Could I play a thief?

The head stylist was chatty and amiable. She led me to the back of the trailer and pulled a heavy curtain behind us.

"Let's see what we have here," she said, medically.

As she examined my dated dresses, a Chihuahua pushed under the curtain and began sniffing my feet.

"That's Humphrey," said the stylist.

Humphrey stared at me. All the humans he encountered smelled like fine leather goods and aioli and macarons. I must be a stray.

"Is he named after Dan Humphrey?"

This, I assumed, was a self-evident question.

The costume designer studied my face, questioning her own judgment in treating me like a person up until this point.

"After Humphrey Bogart."

"Oh." I looked at the dog. "I guess you had him before you started working here."

"I've had him for three months," she said, "but everyone thinks he's named after Dan for some reason."

She pulled the last dress from my bag and called for her assistant.

"This will work," she said. "But tell you what . . . why don't you borrow a pair of these?"

We were flanked by walls of overpriced designer fabrics and tailoring that glimmered at every turn. I peered over her shoulder, anticipating a tray of designer earrings or, say, some very expensive shoes.

She handed me a pair of Spanx.

* * *

I should say that everyone from the director to the actors to the prop stylist was extremely welcoming and kind. Both because it's true and because I should say it. For as small a world as New York is, *Gossip Girl* is even smaller. There are so many people involved with the show, it's rife with awkward intersections that really should not happen in a sane universe. Acquaintances of mine are friends with the cast. The music supervisor used to live in the same building as one of the actors. A friend used to write for the show. Once, I had seen a couple of the stars make out with each other on the swanky sofa of a swanky apartment while I scooted to the edge of the selfsame sofa. It's not that my points of connection are particularly elite. It's that *Gossip Girl* has been filming in New York for exactly the right amount of time to make it a cottage industry. It's the *Law & Order* of my generation, destined to pop up in Broadway *Playbill* bios for years to come.

I did have one very concrete connection to the show, but I didn't want to tell anyone about it. As I walked out of the wardrobe trailer to the van with the blacked-out windows that would drive me to the set, I prayed that Chace Crawford (who plays the show's handsome sheepdog, Nate Archibald) would not be in it. Five years prior I had sat across from Chace at the Empire Diner in Chelsea because a men's magazine had sent me to profile him. I held a microcassette recorder purchased from RadioShack for the occasion, and I watched him order an apple. A whole apple on a little plate. The magazine strongly encouraged me to make him address rumors of his having a romantic relationship with a former NSYNC member. I waited until the end of the interview and, not quite being able to pull the trigger, abruptly asked him to play "fuck, marry, or kill" with three men, one of whom was in a certain boy band, one of whom I can't recall, and one of whom was Burt Reynolds.

"I can't do that," he laughed. He was eager to set the record straight, but not that eager.

"Well, it's that," I said, gesturing at a bulldog tied to a tree outside, "or I ask you to kick that dog."

"Excuse me?"

"Sorry, I'm just trying to think of something you'd rather not do. Sorry again."

"I'm not going to kick a dog, though," he deadpanned.

As we parted ways, I went to hug him. Realizing that ours was not a hug-appropriate relationship, I squeezed his arm instead, using the hand with the tape recorder. It dropped and broke in front of him.

That was the end of the interview.

* * *

When I crawled into the van, Matthew and Kelly were already running lines with each other. Kelly twisted around in the front seat and said hello; Matthew was instantly charming from the back row. I felt like we were all about to go on a field trip. For the briefest of seconds I forgot where I was and thought, Good god, these people look familiar.

"You're the author, right?" said Kelly.

"I'm an author," I said, stating the facts. "I'll be one on the show."

"You write books, though?"

"Yes," I said. "I did."

"But you don't anymore?" Matthew's voice came from the backseat.

"No." I could feel myself being unnecessarily confusing because of my own inability to say the words. "I will. I am. I'm a full-time writer." So I clarified that, yes, "I am the author."

It was the first time since quitting my job that I had said it with such authority. Or at all. I imagine it's the same frame of mind women are in when they tell their manicurist they're pregnant before they tell their own family. Here is a safe space to test out who you are, to see how it sounds. By leaving my career in publishing, I assumed that if I simply eliminated one reality, the remaining one would take over by default. But it turns out that identity is one of those things you have to fight for, even in your sleep.

"So, do you want to run lines with us?" Kelly asked.

"Sure."

"I like your glasses," Matthew said. "I'm in the market for new glasses."

"Who's in here?" came a perky female voice from the open passenger-seat window, saying, "Hi hi hi bye!" before it bounced down the street.

"Who was that?"

"That was Leighton," said Kelly, referring to Leighton Meester, who plays Blair.

I almost stole your bra, Blair.

* * *

I was immediately at ease upon entering the apartment. This was because it was shockingly well scouted, a real ringer for a space in which one might hold an old-school book party. Especially one for a buzzy book. It was a large four-bedroom Upper West Side apartment with lots of quirky oil paintings and dark bookshelves and beat-up area rugs. It looked like the kind of place the editor in chief of an independent publishing house might have bought for $100,000 in 1970. We were ushered down a paper-taped hallway as extras and crew members pressed their backs against the wall. The rest of the actors were already stationed in the living room.

Leighton wasn't in my scene. Nor was Blake Lively (who plays Dan's ex, Serena) or Jessica Szohr (Dan's childhood friend, the biracial daughter of Vermont hippies, whose mom is a dead ringer

for Maya Angelou) or, thankfully, Chace Crawford. But Ed Westwick, the stylish Brit who plays Chuck, was. During the long
breaks between takes, in which the women lay on the master bed
like mummies, lest they ruin their makeup, Ed chatted with concern about riots in London that had been dominating the news.
Then he showed me a video of a horse being hit by a truck on a
country road. The truck plows beneath the horse's legs and the
horse goes flying over the hood of the truck. Magically, he lands
on all fours and trots away. It was violent and horrible and unex-
pectedly funny. I laughed disproportionately. It's possible I said
the words *Oh, that's so wrong.* Kelly opened her eyes on the bed
and raised her eyebrows at me.

I couldn't help it. They were all just so nice, asking me where
I was from, what I wrote, and where I lived. They genuinely
wanted to know about me, a path of conversation that ran in direct opposition to my understanding of the day—that I wasn't
quite me.

"Are you working tomorrow?" Ed asked.

"Yes," I said. "I'm on deadline."

He studied my face. What he meant was: Was I coming back
to the set? It was a lovely misunderstanding, one that made me
feel as if I had temporarily transcended my walk-on complex.
Was I one of them? A natural after all?

By two o'clock we were halfway through filming and I was
starving. In a last-ditch effort to do what a real actress might, I
had skipped breakfast. I assumed Breakfast Pastry Heaven would
await me after shooting. But somehow, either because I missed
seeing craft services while running through the rain or because
the kitchen was filled with sound equipment, I found myself

begging mints off a lighting guy. The prophecy of my line had come to pass: I really was in search of cake.

I nonchalantly expressed a desire for food to Kelly, knowing she is a mom and assuming all mothers know where the closest food is.

"You're hungry?" she asked, mulling the word over. "Huh. I'm not."

This is the kind of digestive narcissism that makes people hate actresses.

Off camera, I eyed the tray of real hors d'oeuvres meant to be part of the background to the party. Once the coast was clear, I quickly consumed a pecan, trying to keep my jaw still and eat at the same time.

"They spray those with poison, you know," said Matthew, who had witnessed my entire operation.

"Yeah, right."

I ate a second nut.

"No, really," he said, gesturing at the spotlights in the corner. "It's so they'll pop on camera."

I spit a little wet pile of masticated nut mess into my palm.

"I'm kidding," he said.

He was a very good actor.

* * *

The actress who played the literary agent and I became friends. We had to stand uncomfortably close to each other for much of the day, because that's how we were blocked. It turned out we lived a street away from each other in real life. While the director spouted off terms I had never heard before, embedded in instructions I was meant to follow right now, she took me under her wing and explained everything to me. She told me when we were rolling, what was practice and what was real. She explained that a "side" was a portion of a script. All the while being directed herself in her first multi-episode role on the show. She would not go back to being some other self tomorrow. This was her real life, her career, her paycheck—and I, the lowly walk-on, was threatening it with dumb questions. Yet she was selfless in her assistance.

To celebrate her inaugural appearance on the show (she appeared in one episode before mine and five after), she had a party at her apartment. Someone handed me a glass of wine and we settled on the couch. As the lights were dimmed, I quickly grilled her about the rest of the party scenes, about what happened to the characters in the days after I left. Late in the game, I had become a *Gossip Girl* addict.

"Whose apartment is it supposed to be, anyway? Your boss's?"

"Mine."

"No, it's not."

"Yes," she insisted, as if it were really hers, "it's my apartment."

"No. That can't be."

With a quick snip, my one tether between reality and *Gossip Girl* was cut. A twenty-seven-year-old literary agent does not live in that apartment. She just doesn't. Even if she's descended from titans of publishing. I didn't need *Gossip Girl* to be realistic about books or writers or parties. Or pretty much anything. The show features a lot of usurping of fashion shows and sabotaging of record deals, for example, and I assume these are not pitch-perfect representations of their respective industries. But there is one realm in which I know too much about the reality to remain silent about the fantasy and that realm is real estate.

After the screening, I walked home, remembering the very last moments of my scene. You can't see it on TV, but what happens is this: I deliver the last of my few lines, excuse myself to hunt for cake, and rush to get off camera as quickly as possible. What with the director, the assistant director, the makeup artist, six cameramen, and so forth, there are about forty people in the living room at any given time. I duck under a boom microphone, squeeze between two cameras, and find myself released into a dining room visible in the background when the show airs.

The room is filled with extras, split into gesticulating clumps. A couple of guests in the corner absolutely light up upon seeing me enter the room. I feel the same comfort I might feel upon entering a party alone and spotting friends. They mouth, "Hello." I wave and whisper, "Hello," back. The camera is still rolling in the next room, but I am no longer acting. I cross over to them, brushing past other extras, who also aren't saying much. I want to find out how I know this couple. Once I arrive, I see their lips are moving, but they are not actually speaking. Their champagne is flat. There is blocking tape at their feet. Embarrassed, I stand there, leaning on bookshelves filled with prop books. It's not me they are happy to see, it's me.

You
Someday
Lucky

MY NEW COWORKER AND HIS WIFE ARE OBSESSED WITH A personality-diagnosing system called the Enneagram, which originated in fourth-century Alexandria and gained popularity in America during the 1970s. They are both from Boulder, the Bennington of the West, so their affinity for a numerically based wizardry system makes sense. It also makes sense if you've never heard of the Enneagram. Studies show that only 15 percent of people already making their own nut milk have heard of it. It's too complicated to be confined to a place where you might have noticed it, like the back page of a magazine. It makes astrology look as precise as a fortune cookie, numerology as helpful as a mood ring. It makes the Myers-Briggs test look like someone ripped it off a cereal box.

One night after work, I go over to their apartment so they can figure out my personality number. This is a fantastically indulgent exercise, like a four-handed massage or group therapy in which only one person's problems are addressed. Over the course of several hours, they ask me all sorts of questions, some personal, some philosophical, some mined from their many books on the subject. Scenarios presented involve hypothetical reactions to crowded parties, animal attacks, solitary confinement, and statements that describe me best. Information that should take years to impart takes minutes. In the end, I will fall somewhere on a scale between one to ten. Though "scale" is not quite accurate. Every personality number is an equal to the next, numerically labeled for ease and not hierarchy. We eat homemade chocolate cake and ice cream from a tub and compare my test results with the Enneagram chart. This is an open circle overlaid with hexagonal shapes. It bears more than a little resemblance to a devil's pentagram.

After much deliberation, the two of them come to the conclusion that I am a nine. They smile because they, too, are nines. Though she is a nine with four tendencies. They look at each other like this is a point of contention in their marriage that has calcified into a private joke. I feel in on the joke, too.

At work the following week, my coworker and I have our first fight over something minor. I interrupt him in a meeting or he interrupts me. He takes credit for my idea or I take credit for his. I undermine his authority or he tramples over mine. The fact that I can't remember tells you just how minor it was. Either way, we are both royally pissed. We had ordered Chinese takeout for lunch but we don't eat it together even though it was my idea to split an order of scallion pancakes and now the pancakes are in his office and I can smell them from here.

"Your behavior," he types from his office next to mine, "makes me think maybe you're not a nine at all."

In our private hippie language, this is the single most cutting thing he could say.

"Then what would you suggest I am?" I type back, loud enough for him to hear me clacking.

"A six."

At his house, we had speculated about the people we knew in common. Our boss was a three. His boss was a four. My coworker's wife was raised by two sevens. It's a miracle she's not in a mental hospital. As far as I know, we don't know any sixes. I have not begun to defend myself when another text bubble appears:

"Hitler was a six."

I mutter an expletive at my screen. Stupid system. Stupid new friends. Who needs them? I take my food out of the bag, grabbing the fortune cookie first. My whole life, I have eaten the fortune cookie first. This is because they're not real dessert and Hitler probably ate his fortune cookies first. I tear open the plastic wrapping just as my coworker knocks on my door frame. Startled, I drop the cookie into a mug of cold coffee, which splatters onto my shirt. We frown together at the drowning cookie. He has come to give me my half of the pancakes, a peace offering.

"Thank you," I say.

"You're welcome," he says, and returns to his desk.

By the time I rescue the cookie, the fortune is blurred and so are the lucky numbers below it. All that's legible, in red ink on the left-hand side, are the words:

You

someday

Lucky

I pin it to the wall until it's dry. Then I stick it in some underutilized crevice of my wallet, where it will remain until I quit my job, leave town to find myself, and lose the wallet in a foreign city. Why, it could be there still.

Such a nine thing to imagine.

If
You
Take
the
Canoe
Out

THE STRONGEST IMPULSE I'VE EVER HAD TO RIDE A BAGGAGE carousel was at the airport in Santa Rosa, California. What we're dealing with is a flat loop, very unassuming, that curls through some rubber curtains. Candy Land to LaGuardia's Chutes and Ladders. At New York airports, you'd have to not care about germs or physics or dignity to ride a baggage carousel. They're made of overlapping metal scales meant to withstand bodily fluids and bombs. Ride one and you might go to airport jail. Probably not. But the idea of jail is never great. Also you might get a tuba dropped on your head. But the Santa Rosa baggage carousel looks like a kiddie ride. Like you could just pop on and glide through the plastic curtains. Maybe a TSA guy gives you a high five and a doughnut hole on the other side. Maybe the whole doughnut. It's California. Anything's possible.

An hour's drive north of San Francisco, the Santa Rosa airport serves the people of California wine country. The building itself is just a sliver of brick that separates the pavement where the cars park from the pavement where the planes park. Inside there's a soda machine, a lost-and-found, and a wall featuring the airport seal: Snoopy the dog, dressed as Amelia Earhart, navigating his doghouse through the clouds. At this advanced point in our aeronautical history, I am not comforted by Amelia Earhart as a mascot, never mind a cartoon of a dog dressed up like Amelia Earhart. And yet I keep coming back. I go to Northern California for the same reason Charles Schulz, Snoopy's creator, went—for the same reason Hunter S. Thompson, M.F.K. Fisher, Jack London, and Mark Twain went—to write. Or, in my case, to try.

There is a fantasy known as "the writing life." Inasmuch as it's any kind of life at all. Or any kind of fantasy at all. The average person will spend more time over the course of his or her lifetime wondering why *marshmallow* is spelled like that than they will wondering how writers write. But at some point, you may have asked yourself: Who gets up early? Who writes standing up? Who unplugs the television and throws it in the closet? I never see musicians get asked about their habits. *Answer: Bad ones?* Same with actors. Not too many hard-hitting questions about line memorization. This is because those artists go public with their craft in a way that gives their audience an inkling of their rehearsal process, of how the sausage gets made. Writers like to keep our sausage in our pants until the last possible second.

Which means, if you're trying to be a writer yourself, there are scant examples of how—and really? This is not a crowd you want to see pantless and typing. Therefore, when it comes to one another, we find it easier to fantasize about location instead. No one believes that using the same pens as Toni Morrison will make you Toni Morrison, but looking at the same view, breathing the same air? It's better than nothing. Which is why we are the most famous for running away from home. You don't have to be rich. You can apply to a writer's colony or sublet your apartment for a week. You can stockpile vacation days, hire a sitter, and go. Anything for a change of scenery, anything for no distractions. Anything for the ideal conditions. We become increasingly particular about our conditions until part of us can't help but think of all the work we'd get done if only we were buried alive.

* * *

I was twenty-four the first time I skipped town to write. I printed out driving directions in Don't Die–point type and drove to my aunt and uncle's cabin in New Hampshire. Summer was ending, the LIFE IS BETTER AT THE LAKE welcome mats were being rolled up on porches across New England. My aunt and uncle were nice enough to hold off on closing up their place so that I might live out my writing fantasy in seclusion. I would be the very picture of a writer. Or at least their very picture of a writer. *Our little John Grisham over here . . .*

When I arrived, a list of cabin instructions awaited me, pinned down by a box of fudge. There were emergency numbers, an explanation of screen doors detailed enough to be understood by future civilizations, and a canoe paragraph that I skipped entirely. I would not be living my life. I would be writing about it.

How did I spend the next six days? I napped at odd hours. I read on the porch but became so hyperconscious of reading on a porch, I moved inside. I tried not to flush the septic toilet. I watched television. I drank an entire bottle of dessert wine. I ate Ritz crackers by the sleeve, glancing incuriously at the nutritional information. I gave myself ultimatums. *You are not allowed to pee until you finish this paragraph. You may not indulge in episodes of* The Real World *unless you write ~~four~~ two pages.* When people stop writing poorly and start not writing at all. I watched cycle after cycle of *America's Next Top Model* and decided that the contestant who solves the "Tyra Mail" clue is the perfect level of smart. *Go to great heights? I bet we're jumping out of an airplane, you guys!* Any smarter than this and you become unhappy.

The morning of my last day, I took what passed for a manuscript down to the end of the dock. I stretched out my arms, ready to work. A duck waddled down the planks after me, stood beside me, and quacked. Oh look, I thought, nature. The duck promptly released a spray of duck diarrhea on my title page. Then it waited to be congratulated. I shooed it away, knocking the entire manuscript into the water in the process. The pages bobbed beneath the dock, white flags of surrender. I instantly accepted these events, maybe even saw them coming. Like when I transport dirty wineglasses from one room to the other, knowing that one will break en route. Or I'll climb a ladder to change a lightbulb and think: This fixture is probably going to fall on my head if I unscrew it too much. And then I do. And then it does.

* * *

For years after that I stayed put in New York, writing during weekends and late nights, dividing my time between my kitchen and my living room. Until one day, when I got a call from my friend Margeaux, telling me she had moved to Russian River, California. I was unfamiliar with Russian River aside from having seen the words paired together on wine labels. I assumed it was just as bucolic as Napa and Sonoma, only less renowned. Like one of Gisele Bündchen's sisters. But I did know Margeaux. She grew up in Berkeley, buying incense by the pound. She owned a dizzying number of sweatshirts with thumbholes in the cuffs and said "hella" a lot. She explained that her new place, perched in the redwoods, was "hella magical" for writing. Was I interested in house-sitting for a week? Reader, I was. Hella magical country houses do not grow on trees. Well, except for this one. Technically, this one did.

After Margeaux retrieved me from the airport, we stocked up on provisions. This included items such as squash, rice cakes, flax cereal, a jar of cashew butter, and a pride of avocados. Since chipmunks had gnawed through Margeaux's bike tires and the closest market was twenty miles away, the bags of groceries that rattled in the back of her car would have to tide me over. The plan was for her to teach me how not to blow up the house, then head down to San Diego for a family wedding. She'd be back in time to drive me to the airport. My only chore was to water her plants with a garden hose. As someone who never gets to use a garden hose, I was thrilled.

We unpacked the food and stood on her porch, taking in the air, listening to her rather irritating wind chime.

"Is that a wind chime?" I asked.

Of course it was a wind chime. It sounded exactly like a wind chime sounds.

That thing would be coming down the second she left.

Tinging aside, Margeaux was right. Her house was a distraction-free zone. There was no television and the Internet only came through in one corner of the porch, where my laptop acknowledged the presence of a network called "KindBud420."

"Friends of yours?" I asked Margeaux, pointing at the screen.

"Oh," she said, gesturing somewhere up the hill, "the neighbors. You won't see them. You won't see anyone if you don't want to."

The following days were some of the more productive of my life. I found in California what I had been looking for in New Hampshire. I wrote for hours, losing track of time. I wrote lying in bed and standing in the kitchen. I wrote outside, holding my pages in place with a steel camping mug, the magic hour light dancing on the rim. Every morning, I walked down to the river to watch the mist rise. This was a walk that made me earn its more idyllic sections by forcing me down a half mile of shoulder-free interstate with blind corners. Truck drivers mistook me for a meth head on a predawn stumble. Their tires spun gravel in my face as they offered colorful epithets from their open windows. I smiled and waved. Nothing could upset me.

Beneath the bridge that stretched over the river, someone had spray-painted: IF IT IS RIGHT, IT HAPPENS. THE MAIN THING IS NOT TO HURRY. NOTHING GOOD GETS AWAY. —JOHN STEINBECK. I stood with my hands on my hips, inhaling through my nostrils, letting the words sink in—though I was not so far gone to California that I didn't imagine how frustrating it would be to run through an airport with John Steinbeck.

* * *

Margeaux called the day before she was supposed to return. Until that moment, I had been only partially aware of a landline. It took me a second to locate the source of the ringing because it was buried under a Mexican blanket.

"Hi," she began, "we have a small problem."

I looked out the window. I may have gotten hose-happy on the plants. But how would she know?

Apparently, Margeaux's great-uncle had a heart attack during the wedding and was taken to the hospital, where he died by the time the reception was over. Margeaux and her great-uncle were as close as that particular relationship generally dictates, but since she was already down there, she felt obliged to stay a few extra days.

"Of course," I said. "Don't give it another thought."

I told her I was happy to live in her house a little longer, which I was. She thanked me and launched into the play-by-play of the wedding. I tried to listen, but as she spoke, I caught the refrigerator out of the corner of my eye. As much as solitude had helped my writing habits, it had terrorized my eating ones. I had not *not* been plowing through cereal as if being dared. I had not *not* eaten five slices of avocado toast on my first day. Last night's dinner was a can of chili garnished with Tostito shards. But I am a grown woman, I thought. I can figure out how to feed myself.

After we hung up, I approached the refrigerator. When I could stand the suspense no longer, I whipped open the door. There were bottles of salad dressing and spreads kept flush by a bar, as if on a condiment roller coaster. There were a couple of eggs, a browning head of lettuce, and something that could no longer reasonably call itself yogurt.

"Crap," I muttered.

Things in the pantry weren't looking much better. I went out to the garden to see if the plants could return the favor. Alas, there was nothing in bloom. I started calculating. I figured I could last about two days before I started stripping bark from the trees and licking it. Margeaux would be home in four. I stood on the porch and leaned on the railing. This was ludicrous. The not-kidnapped among us rarely starve within the walls of an actual house. But twenty miles of twisting trucker-trafficked road stood between me and the closest grocery store.

I tried to distract myself through writing. I knew I could never be one of those people who forgets to eat, but there was always the chance I could be one of those artists who forgets to eat. But it wasn't long before I found myself idly moving my arrow over the little slice of sonar on the corner of my screen. KindBud420. Where exactly was he or she? Or them. A family of KindBuds, maybe. KinderBudens if they were German. Dear God, they could have streusel.

I closed my laptop and catalogued the contents of Margeaux's pantry: baking soda, sugar, flour. There were two eggs in the back of the fridge. Was I willing to part with two precious eggs to make a cake for strangers? What an Anne Frank–ish dilemma. Minor as far as Anne Frank–ish dilemmas go, but still. Also, I didn't have any oil. Maybe I could just use water. This was a bad plan. Was I really going to go banging down a stranger's door in an area where most people displayed multiple BEWARE OF DOG signs?

My stomach growled.

I cracked the eggs into a bowl and poured in what was left of the whiskey.

* * *

Walking through the woods, I felt like a nosy housewife with a casserole. Or like Little Red Riding Hood without the hood, the basket, or the blind confidence. I zigzagged along, holding my cell phone in the air, hoping for a signal. The phone and I registered the house at the same time.

There was a tall wooden fence that circled KindBud420's property. From the fence dangled dozens of mercifully noiseless wind chimes, muted by the angle from which they hung. A row of terracotta frogs glared up at me from the dirt, their mouths agape. I knocked. Nothing. A rusted truck was parked on the lawn. On the passenger seat was the seldom-seen dual subscription to *Maxim* and *Mother Jones*. I knocked again, harder this time. The air exploded with the sound of dogs barking. A male figure yelled at them.

"Hello?" I suggested.

"Who is it?" the voice asked.

I could see his eyes moving back and forth through the slots in the fence. It looked like he was holding a knife.

"I'm your neighbor Margeaux's houseguest and I have cake."

Tonally, this landed somewhere between international spy and "I carried a watermelon."

"Oh!" he said, opening the fence. "Come in, come in!"

Two Yorkshire terriers came running out to lick me.

"I'm Hank."

Hank shook my hand firmly. He was in his late twenties with a reddish goatee and a toothy grin. He held a pair of barbecue tongs. Once inside the house, he called for his girlfriend, Savannah, who emerged from the bedroom in a paisley tunic, all smiles and dreadlocks. They had been expecting me. Why hadn't I come sooner?

"Really?" I asked.

"Margeaux mentioned something last week about maybe having a visitor," said Savannah. "Was it last week, Hank?"

"I think it was last week."

I suppose I, too, would be delighted by guests if I lived in the woods, though my delight would stem from a sense of relief, thus proving that I should not be living in the woods in the first place.

"You brought us a cake!" Savannah exclaimed and hugged me. "We can have it after dinner. Hank, Margeaux's friend brought us a cake."

But Hank was already back to marinating something that smelled delicious.

"Do we know where I put the red wine vinegar?" he asked.

"Did you make this?" Savannah asked, sniffing the brown slab.

"I did," I admitted. "It has whiskey in it. It might be inedible."

Savannah sat me down beneath a beaded map of Tibet and handed me a glass of organic wine. The dogs wheezed on my thighs. I couldn't figure out what either of my hosts did for a living but knew better than to ask such an East Coast question.

Hank grilled sweet potatoes and onions and went outside to check on the salmon.

"Oh," Savannah said, smacking her forehead. "You have to stay for dinner!"

Yes, I really did have to. She plied me with hummus and crackers and dragged me out to their deck. The handful of visible houses all featured elevated decks with tall trees sticking up through them.

"Check it out," Savannah gestured, inviting me to stand on a bench with her.

If you angled yourself at the exact right spot, you could see into Margeaux's kitchen. There was my laptop on the table, surrounded by dirty mugs.

"I've decided to sunbathe the rest of the week. If you're going to stay in that house, you'll basically have no choice but to see me naked."

"I could always avert my eyes."

"Maybe if you see Hank naked."

"Okay," I agreed. "Maybe then."

As I shoved crackers down my gullet like a crazed pelican, Savannah pointed out the sights—where they planned on installing a zip line, their garden shed, their neighbor's house down the hill, which boasted an outdoor hot tub that we could use anytime we wanted, the charred blueprint of a recently exploded meth lab.

"Fucking tweakers," she said, shaking her head. "One tried to break into Margeaux's place before she moved in. Don't tell her that. Hank pulled a shotgun on the guy. Don't tell her that, either."

Hank and Savannah's kindness was rare and overwhelming.

It's easy to go out of your way for a stranger if you know that person is subsisting on cashew butter. But I never revealed my predicament to them. I once attended a wedding where, while expounding his new wife's virtues, the husband explained that she was the first person he'd call if he were ever in a Thai prison. Everyone cooed at this. But all I could think was: That's not love. This isn't to say they didn't love each other, but what a horrible example. When the basic becomes exotic, you're in trouble.

"Dinner's ready," Hank said, poking his head out from the kitchen window.

"I hope you're hungry," Savannah said, putting her arm around my waist.

"Babe," Hank called, "you want to light the incense?"

"I'll do it!" I shouted too loudly.

* * *

They insisted I take home leftovers. I didn't bother with the "I couldn't possibly." I very much could and possibly. In exchange for a wobbly tower of tinfoil shapes, I left them Margeaux's cake pan with a biopsy of the inedible cake cored from the center.

The following day, I went for a hike, casually pulling ripe berries from bushes. On the way back, I heard a sharp laugh coming from the river. I sped up, hopping over tree stumps. I leaned over the bridge to see Hank and Savannah, lounging on inflatable rafts. All of the built-in beverage holders were occupied. It was 10 a.m.

"Savannah!" I shouted, cupping my hands together.

"Did you hear something?" the top of her head said to the top of Hank's head.

"Psssst!"

"What are you *doing* up there?" she asked, as if no one in history had ever walked over a bridge.

"Come down!" Hank shouted.

I practically hurled myself down the hill to greet them. When I stopped sliding, I saw they had company. There was another friend on a third raft, floating beneath the Steinbeck quote. I waded out as far as the seam of my shorts, raising my hand and squinting. This new person was a cousin of Hank's, a DJ with arm-sleeve tattoos and coasters in his ears. I felt a pang of disappointment that I was not Hank and Savannah's only stray.

"Get in, honey," said the DJ. "No one cares."

"I'm not wearing any underwear!" I lied.

Not being in the mood to strip in broad daylight seemed like insufficient reasoning for this crowd.

"Well," said Hank, "this is Alex."

I waved at him. He nodded in return.

"You should come to dinner again tonight!" Hank shouted.

"Oh, you have to!" Savannah said, agreeing so adamantly, she flipped her raft.

* * *

This time I just walked in. Bob Marley was pulsating from tiny speakers on the ceiling. The dogs licked my legs. Hank and Alex were hovering intently over Hank's computer. Alex had removed the coasters from his ears so that his lobes hung in loose slits. There are few things sadder than an off-duty earlobe that's been trained to accommodate a human fist. Alex's forearm muscle moved beneath a pattern of flowers as he lit a cigarette. He looked up at me.

"You wanna bump?"

"I'm good," I said.

I have rarely known drugs to be a predinner activity. Cocaine in particular seemed at philosophical odds with this scene.

"What are you guys looking at?"

I pointed at the computer, assuming either Alex was picking out music or Hank was picking out a recipe.

"Don't show her that!" Savannah said, bursting in from the porch, holding a pellet gun.

"Don't show her what?" I asked.

"Come on," Hank reasoned, "she's cool."

"I'm cool," I said, speaking to the gun that everyone seemed to be taking for granted.

"Oh, get over yourselves," Alex said. "Have a look, honey."

He twisted the laptop around. On the screen was a series of vertical boxes, featuring naked couples. Most were full-body shots but some were only from the waist down and some only from the neck up, smiling and wholesome as wedding announcements. I tried so hard not to look surprised, my pendulum swung too far in the other direction. I nodded at the screen as if these naked couples were not as impressive as the many naked couples I see every day.

"The worst," Hank said, rolling his eyes, "is when Savannah gets a guy with a small dick. You should see some of these tiny dicks."

Should I, though?

"Oh," I said, "I'll bet that sucks."

"Or doesn't at all." Alex snickered and scrolled.

"So," I asked, "you guys are swingers?"

Is that a wind chime?

"We just do pairs," Savannah explained. "It's hard around here. You get a lot of people who are either gross or married or people who have never done this before. I told Hank: Never again with the virgins. Never again."

"Like 9/11," Alex mumbled, wiping his nose.

"That's 'Never forget,'" I said, "but sure."

"Last week," Savannah went on, "this chick freaked out halfway through and locked herself in the closet. I felt kind of bad fucking her boyfriend while Hank had to sit out in the living room."

I gave them a pinched look, as if I, too, hated it when that happened. I imagined Hank waiting patiently, listening to Savannah climax, flipping through worn copies of *Mother Jones.*

"A lot of people don't agree with our orientation," Hank said.

Was it a hobby or an orientation? I wasn't sure it qualified as an orientation unless they *couldn't* have sex without four people in the room.

"She should help you guys look," Alex said and lit a cigarette.

Should she, though?

He held it up by his ear, fingers flared. He saw right through me.

"That's a great idea!" exclaimed Savannah. "How's your eye for labia? Can you smoke that outside please?"

* * *

I was equal parts relieved and insulted to be categorized as someone who could help hunt but not be hunted herself. I did not want to have sex with either of them. Or both of them. But everybody likes to be considered. Instead, I got to work, weeding out couples I suspected were lacking in genetics or experience. Hank diced tomatoes for the bruschetta while I jotted down my favorite pairings on a notepad.

Laura and Craig. Her: 5′2″, 119 lbs, boobs. Him: 6′1″, 170 lbs, bald.

Diana and Jay. Her: 5′7″, 130 lbs, flat. Him: height N/A. 140 lbs. Jockey?

"Too little." Savannah stood over my shoulder, licking a wooden spoon.

"Which one?"

"Him. The bald guy."

"Not the jockey?"

"It says he's a jockey?"

"That's just what I'm calling him."

"Well, your jockey has a ginormous cock. Look at him. He's hung like a horse."

"How can you tell?" I asked. "It's just his face."

"You get good at reading people," she said, shrugging. "Everyone's always trying to tell you something. It's in their eyes. It's not that hard."

"Man." I kept scrolling. "You're good."

* * *

"I can't." Hank waved his hands back. "I can't with the pancake nipples."

We were eating dinner outside, breathing in the cool forest air and trolling the Internet for nipples of an acceptable diameter.

"What would you go for?" Savannah asked. "If you were us."

"Me?"

All I could think about were logistics. I wondered how long it took to get a response from the couples, if they all took each other out to dinner afterward, if they split the check four ways. The three of them were waiting for an answer. I tried to imagine what the newfangled Northern Californian version of myself would say. Days working alone, deep in thought, had left my mind uncluttered and unusually prepared to access thoughts on the subject.

"I guess I'd go for something traditional," I mused. "So a girl with a distinct figure and long hair and a tall guy with chest hair. Or I'd focus on diversity so there's one of everything in the room. It leads to less whose-ass-is-that and so forth. Conversely, I could see hunting down a set of body doubles to make the transition more seamless. But if the whole idea is to go outside the relationship, then what's the point of that?"

Alex lit up another cigarette. The paper crackled.

"Precisely," Hank whispered.

Was I a foursome savant? I'd never been so flattered in my life. A foursome is one of those activities that lives in the "would" section of my brain alongside "black tar heroin" and "petting a baby cobra." Would I do these things? Sure, if the circumstances were perfect and consequence free and came with a bucket of antivenom.

* * *

After dinner, we marched into the woods, single file, because Savannah and Hank had a surprise for me. I felt out of my body, as if narrating my evening from the trees: Unbeknownst to her loved ones, a writer befriends her sexually liberated neighbors and allows herself to be escorted to a dilapidated garden shed. Her would-be assailants roll her a joint the circumference of a giraffe turd. So relieved is she not to list her current activity as "being stabbed" that she does not hesitate to take it. Inside the shed is a creaky staircase that leads to the center of the earth.

The stairs opened up into a space more expansive than I had expected. I heard the dull buzzing of a generator. Hank flicked on a series of infrared lights. And there, underneath Hank and Savannah's backyard, was a greenhouse hosting the tallest marijuana plants I'd ever seen. I am not a weed aficionado. I am not an anything aficionado. But I know what a normal-size pot plant looks like and they don't crown at your armpit. This was what the dinosaurs smoked.

Hank turned on a fan. The leaves shivered in the breeze. He guided his hand over them, as if calming them.

"We do a couple hundred thousand dollars a year," he boasted.

"You want some?" Savannah asked, chewing on a dread. "We can send you some."

"Just a couple of ounces," Hank clarified. "Margeaux will give us your address."

Margeaux probably would do such a thing. When she returned from San Diego I would tell her everything about my *Bridges of Sonoma County* weekend. I would tell her I was starving and wound up trolling through a catalogue of scrotums with the neighbors. She wouldn't even flinch.

"I don't want to trouble you," I said. "I can always sneak some in my luggage."

I had no intention of doing that either.

"It's no trouble," said Hank. "I ship it all the time. I seal it in duct tape."

The truth is I am not a big weed person. I say this as someone who has given it more than its fair share of chances. In return, it often makes me paranoid, stupid, and prehuman. If weed and I were dating, it would be one of those on-and-off relationships that goes on for years, the kind that usually ends with one of us in a bathtub at 4 a.m., saying, "My feet hurt, let's get nachos."

"Let's go upstairs." Savannah removed a bag from a temperature-controlled humidor. "Hank refuses to smoke in front of the plants."

She rolled her eyes.

"Would you eat meat in front of a cow?" he asked me.

I would not. But I had also never been to a restaurant that offered.

* * *

Alex had put his earrings back in. Savannah blew smoke through his lobes. I was instantly, embarrassingly, uncontrollably high, but in a more delightful way than expected. Delightful to me, at least. I took a corner of the blanket and rolled myself up in the style of a human croissant. I could feel a layer of myself separating from the rest of me like the sole of a worn shoe. Hank squinted at me in the dark.

"What are you laughing at?"

"I'm not laughing," I said.

"You are."

"I can see up all your noses," I announced, lying on my back like an overturned bug. "You know what word you don't hear enough of? *Cilia*."

"You're coming with me," Savannah said, steadying one of my ankles to keep it from hitting her in the face.

* * *

Never having owned a hot tub, I didn't realize they could be locked. I assumed they just got covered in trash bags to prevent woodland creatures from falling in and that was that. Apparently, what one does is purchase a zippered cover, put a padlock on the zipper, crisscross the entire tub in wire, and tie the wire in a knot.

"Are you sure your neighbors are okay with this?" I whispered.

I took a sip from my wineglass, which I had brought with me, like a blankie.

"Yeah," Savannah said, waving me away. "I do it all the time."

She fiddled with the wire knot, bending down so that her tunic gaped open to reveal her braless chest. A motion-sensitive light turned on, attracting moths.

"Hey," I spoke to the ground, "when's the last time you saw me with shoes?"

She was growing frustrated.

"I can't get this thing open."

"Here," I said, setting my drink down, "let me do it."

She stood upright with her hands on her hips, hovering above me while I leaned down and pretended to listen for clicks in the padlock wheel.

"Do you know what you're doing?"

During college, I used to cram a dining hall pass into my door frame when I forgot my keys. This was the extent of my lock-picking expertise.

"You're blocking the light," I said. "I can't see."

"I thought you were listening."

"I'm doing both."

"Do you know what might help?" she whispered. "Pliers."

"Pliers," I agreed, "or permission."

"I *have* permission," she insisted. "I do this all the time."

Just then a popping sound ripped through the air. It whistled over our heads like a comet rustling through the braches. If wildlife scampered, I didn't notice. Probably because I was distracted by the sound of someone trying to kill me. Savannah and I hit the deck just as an authoritative male voice called down from the porch.

"Goddamnit, Savannah!"

Was everyone handed a shotgun when they bought property around here? Savannah and I hid behind the wall of the tub, legs forward as if we had been wounded on the battlefield.

"Are we gonna get murdered now?" I whispered, trying not to laugh.

"Nah," she said, "it's too dark to get murdered."

My hazy mind instantly accepted this logic. Even if it hadn't,

I was in Savannah's hands now, living by the rules of her territory. Which felt like my territory too, a hella magical place of weed and creativity and pancake nipples. It's easy to be dismissive of people like Savannah from a distance, specifically the three thousand miles of gradating culture that separates New York from California. For New Yorkers, the assumption is that, given a Xanax and a hammock, we could survive in their world, but they could not survive in ours. But I have rarely known New Yorkers who are as up for anything as Hank and Savannah.

"I know you're out there!" cried the hot tub's owner, firing another shot straight up into the air.

"You do this all the time, huh?"

"Some of the time," she admitted. "Twice."

"Should we?" I mouthed, making my fingers run in the air.

Savannah shook her head no. We listened to the crunch of her neighbor pacing back and forth on dry pine needles. It sounded like the marching of an entire army. At long last, he gave up and went inside the house. Savannah turned to whisper something soothing in my ear, but I will never know what it was because I was already gone. The second I heard that screen door slam, I bolted into the night, barefoot, back to Margeaux's house, and locked the door behind me.

* * *

When the package arrived at my apartment three weeks later, there was no return address. Just a stamp, narrowing the origin to Russian River, California. I stood in my cramped entryway and leaned against the row of corroded mailboxes. I ripped the package open, sending my nose in first like a weed canary. Hank wasn't kidding. It smelled like the inside of a padded envelope. At the bottom was a small bundle wrapped in layers of packing tape.

Once inside my apartment, I turned the envelope upside down. I was excited at the prospect of a souvenir, a symbol that those days had really happened. Mostly, I just wanted to smell it. But the bundle made a surprising thud. As I tore it open, I heard the contents before I saw it: a miniature version of Margeaux's wind chime along with a note from her that read, "A little something to remember the country by. Ps. Have you seen my cake pan?"

I lifted the wind chime in front of my face, holding it by its tail like a dead mouse. Out of some sense of duty, I hung it from the fire escape, where it blathered away in the breeze, mocking my inability to ignore it. I tried to push through the sound as I wrote, rereading the same paragraph over and over again, attempting to will myself into a California state of mind. Hank and Savannah wouldn't let themselves be perturbed by a wind chime. Then again, there were a lot of things that Hank and Savannah would do that I wouldn't. I was not new me. I was parallel me. And parallel me lasted approximately thirty seconds before flinging open the window, ripping that thing down, and getting back to work.

The Chupacabra

LOCALS IN VERMONT HAVE SPOTTED AN ANIMAL THAT THEY believe to be a chupacabra, a mythical South American creature said to feed on the blood of goats. Witnesses have seen it wandering through farms and graveyards, its skin blistered, its eyes possessed. While the chances of it being a rabid dog are good, no one is ruling anything out. So a magazine sends me up north to see if I can find it. I am a less-than-ideal candidate for the job. I don't specialize in mythical-creature hunting or even run-of-the-mill hunting. But the unspoken point of the enterprise is not to find the chupacabra, but to find myself instead, to make a larger point about the power of the imagination, to discover a tick on my shin after traipsing through the woods. Won't that be fun?

I spend two unfruitful days stalking animals that turn out to be deer or, in one case, a rusted car. At the end of the second day, I return to my roadside motel and collapse onto my bed face-first. Having covered what feels like most of southern Vermont on foot, I limp over to a black binder on the coffee table. Inside is a series of laminated advertisements for pizzerias and diners, tourist attractions and kid-friendly activities. On the last page, there's a small square. Printed in Comic Sans (is there any other kind?) inside the square is the word *Relax!* and a number for Fran, a "24-hour masseuse." It's hard to reconcile the childlike font with the adultlike "24-hour masseuse." But I decide to give it a shot, reasoning that I can always leave if it turns out Fran and I are on different wavelengths. I call the number. She's just had a cancellation and so I drive to the address listed in the ad. Which, as it turns out, is her house.

A slight, cheerful woman in an apron answers the door. When I guess her name, she corrects me. She is Fran's housekeeper, finishing up for the day. She escorts me to a paisley love seat in the living room where I can wait for Fran. The room is wood paneled, with wall-to-wall carpeting and shelves that sag with the weight of self-help books. A large flat-screen TV is showing a reality-television series I'm too old to recognize. A geriatric Maltese by the name of Chartreuse, according to her collar, pants at my feet. Chartreuse is afflicted with an excessively crooked neck, which the housekeeper informs me is the result of one too many seizures. The white fur around her eyes is stained with years of gook so that her eyes resemble quotation marks. Like she's only sarcastically a dog. She moves back and forth across the room, an inquisitive puppet.

After several commercial breaks, Fran emerges in pink slippers, a pink muumuu, and pink latex gloves.

"How is your evening?" Fran asks, by way of a hello.

She invites me to follow her so that we can select some invigorating oils together. The housekeeper takes my place on the sofa, intently watching a young woman on TV wearing a microphone bigger than her bikini ease into a hot tub. The woman announces that the hot tub is hot. I trail Fran down a hallway, to the massage room, quickly adding up all the people who know where I am.

Fran instructs me to get undressed and shuts the door, leaving me alone. The room is lined with china figurines inspired by the major motion picture *Misery*. I lie down, pulling the sheet back, adjusting my head in the massage table's head-doughnut. Fran enters the room, lowers the lights, and douses me with enough oil to alert the EPA. Then she gets to work. Within seconds, I know this will be the best massage I've ever had. Fran's pressure is perfect, her fingers homing in on the muscles in need. She cleans the knots out from beneath my shoulder blade as if she were sweeping leaves from a gutter. I begin to drift off, thinking of the elusive chupacabra, thinking the solipsistic thought that there's not much of a difference between no one finding it and it never existing.

I am brought back to consciousness by the sound of heavy panting. I open my eyes to see that not only has Chartreuse meandered into the room, but she has settled herself into my field of vision. Fran must have left the door open a crack.

"Hi," I mouth.

Chartreuse pants while I stare, unblinking, into her eyes. You're not supposed to stare animals directly in the eye for a prolonged period of time, but what's she going to do to me from all the way down there? She proceeds to have a full seizure as I look down, my cheeks crammed into the headrest. Her body shakes. Her ears go in different directions. I am unclear on the etiquette here. Fran says nothing as Chartreuse keels to her side and shakes, her limbs going stiff. It looks like she's trying, and failing, to break-dance. Still, Fran stays mum. She moves methodically down my spine as if nothing is happening. Because, for her, nothing is. She sees this kind of thing all the time. But me, I don't move a muscle, because I have never seen anything like it.

Up
the
Down
Volcano

APPARENTLY, ECUADOR IS GRACED WITH ALL FOUR SEASONS IN the course of a single day, and so I pack for none. Instead, I throw a random selection of clothing in a small duffel bag, stuffing a bikini and a fleece vest into the pocket of negative space that appears when I zip it. A sense of satisfaction washes over me as I force-feed nylon straps through plastic teeth. There's no reason for me to feel satisfied. You need many more items than the ones I have chosen for a day at the beach or a circumnavigation of Greenland. But I have made a habit of underpacking, of escorting aspirational accessories around the globe as if they were children on a disastrous family trip.

"You wanted to see Miami?" I put a straw hat on a glass coffee table where it will stay untouched until I repack it. "There, now you've seen it."

My aversion to overpacking and its uptight cousin, overplanning, stems from the belief that neither tendency is a fake problem. These are not amusing tics. They are instead reflections on the personality of the packer. They suggest a dubiousness of other lifestyles (racist), a conviction that the world won't have what you need (princess), and a lack of faith that you'll continue being human when it doesn't (misanthrope). And how hard is it, really? I think by now we can all agree that the foundation of world travel goes something like "Bring a cardigan."

Thusly armed with my meager tributes to a four-in-one climate, I lift my bag. My bicep aches from yesterday's visitors: a series of offensively long needles. I am off to Quito, the capital of Ecuador, because a travel magazine has told me to go there. My nebulous mission is to wander around the city for a few days, interact with locals, and write about it. It's a dream assignment for anyone and I have never been to South America. Thus, I find it to be extra dreamy.

Because I am the temporary ward of a media company, I am advised to seek out multiple inoculations, including one for typhus. It's all fun and games until someone gets typhus. I am also encouraged to pick up a prescription for malaria pills should I venture farther afield. Quito isn't Tokyo, no, but it's a major city with running water. The quotidian equivalent of such precautions would have me being one of those people who spray hand sanitizer on subway poles.

"Is this really necessary?" I ask my editor, who points out how difficult things will be for me if I get sick and can't communicate.

"You don't speak Spanish."

"I hablo un poco de espan-yoal," I defend myself.

"Uh-huh," he says.

* * *

Few instances in my life have made me feel so tough as helping the Duane Reade pharmacist locate my malaria pills.

"What are we looking for, hon?" she shouts over her shoulder, thumbing her way through a bin of pills and creams for normal-people problems.

Chain-store pharmacists put exactly as much effort into patient privacy as I do into packing. Until they invent a Libido Dampening syrup or a capsule for Being Too Darn Pretty, this will be the only time I'll proudly announce the contents of my envelope to all the land. A line forms behind me. I feign shyness at the impressed glances of my fellow customers. They wouldn't have pegged me as a war photographer or an aid worker but oh, how wrong they are.

Both the pills and the shots wind up bolstering my sense of adventure, my desire to take my body out for a spin. As if I am dealing with extra minutes on a phone plan, not my immune system. Use it or lose it! I wish I could apply this attitude to my daily life, but I'm a lazy person within the confines of New York City. I won't meet a friend more than ten blocks from my apartment if it's too windy and the sidewalks are looking especially hard today.

I am skeptical of ferries and bus transfers. Often I will walk past a restaurant and have the thought: *I should order out from there later.*

But the whole point of this trip is to leave it to chance. Well, chance and Facebook. Unlike casting a social net for tips on Dublin or Buenos Aires, where comment after comment would compete in an e-thumb war for supreme regional wisdom, people are content to deliver their advice regarding Quito in direct messages. Few have spent quality time there. Three people chime in. One suggests a restaurant with fruit drinks, one suggests a museum with paintings of skeletons, and the third suggests I climb Cotopaxi, a 20,000-foot active volcano. Dubious of the Wi-Fi in my budget hotel (racist), I type up the list in advance: fruit drink, skeleton paintings, active volcano. Got it. I hold the list in my hand as I lock my apartment door. Each activity seems equally viable. Looking back, I think it's because they were all in the same point-size type.

* * *

Now feels like as good a time as any to mention that I've never been skiing. You have to be under four feet tall to see the appeal of skiing. When you're a kid, there are magic bravery crystals on the surface of the snow that whisper, telling you it's fun to go speeding down nature's backbone as if it won't kill you. After a certain age, you become too tall to hear the crystals. So by the time you're an adult, the question "Want to go skiing next weekend?" actually sounds like "Want to go bungee jumping using this old dental floss I just found?" The big selling points for ski trips, or the ones most regularly paraded out for my unskilled benefit, are mugs of warm liquid. Wait. Let me get this straight: While all my friends exercise, bond, and embrace the outdoors, my reward for a hard day of solo snowman crafting is more hot chocolate? To what do I owe this glut of me-time? Maybe later, when I grow bored of lying on rugs, I can wander into town and spin postcard racks. No, no winter sporting expeditions for me, thank you.

Upon arriving in Quito, I solicit the advice of my hotel's Peruvian receptionist, a shock-pretty university student whose affections I like to think I have won. This I have achieved by waiting patiently while other guests ask stupid questions and then asking brilliant ones of my own. Like how to flush the toilet in my room. When not manning the front desk, booking expeditions to the Galápagos Islands, the receptionist likes to climb mountains. This turns out to be common in Quito. The capital is located in a goose pot of one of the most densely collected circles of peaks on the planet, including Cayambe, Cotopaxi, the fun-to-say Pichincha, and the fluid-looking Imbabura, with its mystical importance. The Incas used to worship it. Imbabura is Zen in rock form. It's also not the one I intend to climb.

When I tell her of my interest in climbing Cotopaxi, a massive landform I apparently can't be bothered to google, she seems unfazed. She went last month. The volcano has a symmetrical crater like a punch bowl in clouds. It's one of the most stunning things she's ever seen. Why wouldn't I go? Looking at a photograph of her and her boyfriend tacked to the wall behind her— both of them wearing head-to-toe North Face and holding up ice axes from which all the power of the universe emanates— I decide to play up my ignorance.

I explain that I am a novice climber, by which I mean very. It's a miracle I haven't spontaneously fallen to the floor in the time we've been speaking. I point at her phone and encourage her to pull up a photograph of the mountain I used to hike every summer in New Hampshire. It's the most frequently climbed mountain in North America. I was nine years old the first time I went up. I used to play freeze tag on the summit.

"Is the mountain on the next page?"

She is genuinely confused, moving the screen closer to her face, trying to broaden the image with her fingers.

"Exactly," I say.

Convinced of my greenness, she knows just the person to escort me up the mountain, a friend of hers named Edgardo. Edgardo is a professional mountaineer, in that sometimes apparel brands send him parkas. Which is good enough for me, as I have been sent no parkas. He doesn't usually do beginner tours but he "is a climber who is a very good climber."

A few phone calls later and Edgardo is set to arrive the next morning. He has agreed to take me up Cotopaxi for a reasonable fee. At this point I know so little about mountain climbing that I don't think I'm skimping by avoiding a more official expedition. Actually, it's the reverse—I reason I must be paying more than normal to limit my stranger quotient. In fact, before she suggested Edgardo, I asked the receptionist if I couldn't just handle the trip on my own. I had designs on trading the forced loneliness of nonfluency for the intentional loneliness of nature immersion. I imagined glacial streams and wildflowers, salamanders and roots. Whatever I thought, it has since been corrected. Painted over. Like *Dogs Playing Poker*.

* * *

When Edgardo shows, I am sitting in silence with the few other foreign guests dotting the spare hotel dining room. The soft morning light shines through the spikes atop the security gate outside. I am pretending to read a Spanish newspaper and polishing off a breakfast of corn and eggs, when a petite man darts across the room wearing what appears to be the mountain climber's answer to the scuba suit. A coarse braid of hair swings over one of his shoulders. The braid is so thin at the end, I am amazed its owner managed such a delicate procedure.

Edgardo carries with him a strappy backpack and plops himself down across from me. My coffee sloshes onto the table. I can feel it drip through the cracks in the wood and onto my knee. But I sit still, holding the newspaper, using it as a shield. Every set of eyes in the room watches Edgardo lean back in the chair like he owns it.

"Is your name Sloane?"

No.

"Yes."

"Do you eat beans?"

This is one of maybe five questions Edgardo will ask me in the entire time I know him. The first being the confirmation of my name. I nod.

"Good," he says. "I'll get the things and we meet outside in one hour."

And that is the longest string of English I'll hear from Edgardo. It's as if he memorized it for effect, same as if the only sentence I knew how to say in Spanish was "This remote control only takes double-A batteries."

"Okay," I say.

He pushes his chair back from the table.

"One hour," he repeats, holding up his pointer finger in a stern fashion as if he knows I have an issue with lateness. Because I do, in fact, have an issue with lateness, this otherwise rude assumption has a positive impact. I feel like Edgardo and I have known each other forever.

"Got it," I say.

"Oh." Edgardo stops himself and removes a pair of mountain-climbing boots from his backpack. "We need to understand your feet."

He drops to the ground as if about to propose and grabs my ankle. A couple at the next table looks the other way. Despite their clunky shape, the boots are too small. We'll have to add "boots" to the list of things to rent before we go—a list that evidently includes crampons, a Gore-Tex jumpsuit, and a headlamp. I am starting to detect the faintest odor of intensity to all this.

"Is what I'm wearing okay?"

I push back from my chair and wipe crumbs off my lap. I am wearing cotton tights and a pilled tank top. It's less of an outfit than a few swaths of cloth to carry me from my room to a public dining room in a socially acceptable fashion.

"Yes, yes," he says. "One hour."

I go back to my room and locate the warmest clothing I can find, which amounts to the fleece vest. I lock my passport in a counterintuitively communal safe, operated by a janitor. Then, just as I'm getting ready to leave, I feel an ache in my abdomen. I go to the bathroom to find that there's both a Coto*maxi* joke *and* a crampon joke to be made—but no one around to get it.

* * *

Edgardo arrives outside the hotel three hours later. When he pulls up, I see that his Jeep features an orange-and-red flame extending from door to bumper and blacked-out windows. He fusses with a tarp on top of the Jeep, pulling hard at ropes. When I ask him if I can help, he says nothing. When I ask him if he's sure I can't help, he tells me I should get in the car—but not before looking me up and down and asking: This is what you wear?

I open the passenger door, expecting the car to be empty. But a second man reclines in the back of the Jeep. It would seem the "we" that needed to understand my feet was not royal but literal. This second man I will come to know as Pedro. Pedro's primary contributions to our journey include pointing out gas stations, eating massive quantities of fruit, sleeping with his arms crossed, and pulling off Oakleys. He nods as I climb into the passenger seat. A small hill of orange peels at my feet, along with a warmth emanating from my seat fabric, tells me that Pedro's perch in the backseat is a recently acquired one.

"That's my assistant," Edgardo explains over my shoulder.

Both of them laugh. I know in my heart the joke is about their friendship and not my soon-to-be-unsolved murder case, but my unease regarding a second person operates on two levels. The first is the one in which I'm in no mood to be kidnapped in a foreign country. The second is the one in which I refuse to pay double. It's hard to say which is more pressing. I sit in the car as Edgardo straps supplies to the roof. A first-aid kit comes loose and pops open. The windshield is showered with plastic matches and energy bars. Band-Aids flutter and stick to the glass. Edgardo and I lock eyes. He smiles, picks up a six-inch hunting knife, and shoves it back into the bag.

Trips up Cotopaxi work like this: First, you drive out of Quito, a city whose traffic patterns mirror those of a cubist painting. Once on the outskirts of town, it's another few hours to the base of Cotopaxi. During this time, there are many road types at your disposal. Wide ones, short ones, narrow ones, steep ones, *long, straight, curly, fuzzy, snaggy, shaggy, ratty, matty, oily, greasy, fleecy, HAIR!* Anyway. You will find one road so bumpy, you'll want to keep your jaw ajar so your teeth don't chatter. Boxy pastel houses are sprinkled on the hills in the distance. Soon the towns decrease in size. The crumbling apartment buildings fade from view. The clotheslines become less and less covered in clothes. Keep on vibrating up a "road" whose air quotes grow increasingly pronounced. Try not to listen as your bladder curses the day you dragged it into this world. Hold on to the handle above your window and—hey, watch out for that donkey!—swerve your vehicle straight into a river. Stop the car. Realize it's not really a river you're in, but a swamp saved from stagnation by an open sewage pipe. Lift any electronics off the car floor because you're about to open your door into bacteria-infested rain-forest water. Quickly come to understand that you weigh exactly enough to be of use by exiting the car but too little to be of use pushing it back onto the road.

So just stand there for a while. Distract yourself from whatever it is that just bit your neck by humming the theme song to *Family Ties*. Realize that you know only two lines of this song and one of them is "sha-la-la-la." Once back in the car, go through the gate to Cotopaxi National Park. From here, it's a short drive to the last patch of land not at a 90-degree angle from the earth. Park the car and hike up to a cabin located 15,700 feet above sea level. Upon arrival, eat as much as you possibly can before the altitude destroys your appetite. Then make sure you're asleep by 7 p.m. so that you can wake up five hours later and hike to the summit before the sun rises, melting the path out from under you.

Now, I have to assume that much of that reads as par for the course for an experienced climber. I wouldn't know. I was not she and the decision to spend thirty-six hours up a glacier-encrusted mountain instead of bargaining for alpaca scarves had been a minor one. But even if I had gone the scarf route, the constant state of newness in a foreign country lends a little drama to everything. Even the maiden operation of a local ATM demands problem-solving. It becomes increasingly difficult to parse personal adventure from objective adventure, until you're certain everything should be a challenge, every path a learning curve. It is only later that someone native to the region hears you decided to ride a bicycle to the airport, laughs, and says: Not that steep of a curve.

* * *

Lush green hills look patchy and weighted down. Drops of rain pelt my forehead from a crack in the Jeep's window. We have under an hour to go, according to Edgardo. This is a relief as Edgardo's musical taste leans toward German rap, which, for reasons that will be apparent to anyone who has heard German rap, makes me feel less like we're on a road trip and more like we're in a postapocalyptic novel. The music doesn't stray too far from this genre except for a few plays of Ace of Base's "The Sign," a track I pretend holds emotional significance in order to get Edgardo to skip it.

Twenty minutes later, Edgardo pulls off the highway without warning, stops the car, and runs away on foot. Perhaps this is normal. Perhaps Americans are unnecessarily diligent about telling each other where we're going all the time. If I hear a funny noise in the engine, I say, "Do you hear that?" I don't just stop the car, get out, and leave everyone inside thinking I've embarked on a one-man game of Chinese fire drill. Or if you and I are having a discussion at a party and I have to go to the bathroom, I excuse myself. I don't dart off like a startled horse. I'm not the kind of person who's going to, say, pull over unannounced and go searching for weed in a random village while an overly inquisitive but otherwise tolerable American tourist waits in my car.

I have no idea what this little pit stop has to do with getting to Cotopaxi. Pedro popped out of the vehicle almost as fast as Edgardo, so he's not even here to give me inscrutable looks. The gas tank is full. Maybe it's not weed. Maybe Edgardo has to pick up a quilt his grandmother made him or something. I look around. The landscape outside features chickens, torn advertisements for soda, men leaning against walls, and shirtless children. A soldier strolls by with a large gun strapped to his back.

I push down on the door lock. Then I pull it up again.

I shut my eyes. When I was four years old I came down with pneumonia and hallucinated that my room was packed with bees.

To avoid getting stung, I took refuge in the safest place I knew: under the covers. But of course there were bees there as well. Being inside or outside of the Jeep feels like the same kind of choice.

Bored, I open the glove compartment to find a pile of scratched CDs, ratty gloves, and some travel-size spray cologne. I pick up the cologne. It has the silhouette of a boob on it and rust on the bottom and I am not even tempted to remove the cap. I get out of the car and lean on it, which makes me feel like a prostitute but I don't mind. I reason that prostitutes seem more in control than already kidnapped women locked in a car. A chicken runs by with a couple of kids following behind. Easily distracted from her own survival, the chicken stops to peck at a half-eaten paper plate of food.

When Edgardo and Pedro finally return, Edgardo succinctly instructs me to get back in the car and tosses a large bottle of water on my lap. Quito is not Tokyo, no, but it is not Khartoum, either. There is absolutely no way it takes this long to locate bottled water. I raise one eyebrow at him. If drugs have been introduced to this vehicle, I think I've earned some.

"Drink," he says, adding, as I open the bottle, "you will need on the mountain."

I pull the bottle from my lips like it's poison.

"Do I drink the water now or do I not drink the water now?"

"Now drink," he says, starting the car.

I unscrew the cap again.

"Drink on the mountain."

I have seen many films with scenes like this. I don't need to be part of one myself. If *Cast Away, 127 Hours, Alive, Touching the Void,* and *Panic Room* have taught me anything, it's that you should never leave home without a lighter, a bottle of Gatorade, and a Swiss Army knife. At this point, people who do leave the house without an EpiPen basically deserve what's coming to them. But the survival stuff is never the worst part of these movies. The worst part is those innocuous scenes, before the epic journey, the ones that appear to have nothing to do with anything. Chop off my arm, feed me butt cheek, lock me in a room with Jodie Foster—these will never be the moments that move me as a viewer. It's when our hero or heroine thinks longingly of some basic household staple that my stomach lurches. Nothing is so gruesome to the human imagination as regret.

I drain the bottle down to the plastic rib equidistant between the top and the bottom.

Soon there are no more towns to be found and no more donkeys to be avoided. We drive over lava-worn ground. Wild dogs appear from nowhere and run after the car, barking. It starts to rain harder. The sky blends into the clouds blends into the ice blends into the rocks. Cold air whips through a crack in the dashboard. I worry about my clothing. But if I ask too many questions, Edgardo tells me to be "*tranquilo*." He isolates the word for effect, simply saying "calm," not bothering with the "yourself." I know nothing about Ecuadorian culture, but I'm betting that treating a woman like a hysteric for asking about long underwear does not go over well.

"Pichincha." Edgardo points across my chest, breaking the silence.

"I see," I say.

Pedro reaches silently through from the backseat and offers me pistachio nuts. I shake my head. He shrugs and keeps eating.

We park the car at an adobe-style house complete with a stone path. It's bare-bones, but at this point any evidence of human intent registers as luxurious. We haul our belongings—which for me includes a backpack stuffed with an old sleeping bag of Pedro's, climbing equipment, beans, and a chocolate bar—over our shoulders. I push a wooden door and poke my head into the house. I see a musty rug, a small kitchen, and a ladder leading up to a floor covered in hay. It's somehow colder inside than out and smells of mildew. Pedro comes in behind me. He looks up at the rafters, puts his hands on his hips, and whistles appreciatively.

Edgardo appears behind us.

"We cannot stay here."

"Looks fine to me," I say, fishing in my pack for toilet paper.

I am fond of this role reversal.

"We must go to the refuge," he says plainly and glares at Pedro, who should know better.

Apparently, we are trespassers. This little hacienda is not our destination. It costs quite a bit of money to rent and other people have done that already. This evening's destination is another 1,200 feet up and we will be climbing there on foot. The only reason we stopped here is because Edgardo thought this might be a good spot to layer up.

I unfurl two pairs of snow pants, a sweater, and my fleece vest from my backpack but I am having trouble with the boots. Exasperated, Edgardo grabs my leg, one hand behind the knee and the other on the boot, quickly forcing me to sit on a stone bench. He starts lacing up the boots for me. This would verge on maternal if it weren't the most violent corset-style lacing session of all time. I don't know what kind of mother Edgardo had. Mine used to take a heart-shaped cookie cutter to my peanut butter and jelly sandwiches.

* * *

"Here is where we get out," Edgardo says, firmly.

It's beyond me how anyone could discern "parking space" from where we've stopped. The rain has turned to snow that comes from beneath the car as much as from above it. No one expected a snowstorm but apparently this one doesn't look so bad. I am awash with the impulse to be back in New York in my apartment, imagining it in mid-July when it's too hot to go outside and the first sign of rain is a hollow tapping on the air-conditioning unit. I am freezing already, a fact that Edgardo can't quite believe, despite the purple hue of my lips. I have been backed into trusting him through circumstance. Like a doctor–patient relationship, no matter how extreme my doubt, he is the only one to tell me what's normal. The closest second opinion is five hours and 5,000 vertical feet away. I unbuckle my seat belt. I think that I have never been so cold in my life but try to rid myself of thoughts like this. There's nowhere to go but up.

"Your hands are too cold," Edgardo observes as he watches me not get out of the car.

I am vigorously rubbing my palms together. I would stick them in my mouth if I wasn't worried about the consequences of them being wet when I removed them. Edgardo reaches across me to open the glove compartment. I want to hug him for warmth. This is hard to reconcile, since the more I get to know Edgardo, the less I want to hug him in general. Maybe what I really want is to gut him Jack London–style and use his kidneys for mittens. We smile politely at each other. He pockets the can of cologne. I'm not sure whom he's planning on attracting in a frozen volcano crater. Pedro, meanwhile, goes bounding out of the car, all joints and momentum. The prospect of warmth moves me to follow him. I heave my backpack on and try to keep up.

Edgardo yells after Pedro to slow down. I am like an animal too stupid to know to do this myself. Like those parakeets who have to have their cages covered so they know it's time to sleep. I don't know it yet, but with no climbing experience and less than twenty-four hours at 10,000 feet above sea level, I will most likely pass out from speed-hiking. But right now I feel okay, almost chatty, for a whole minute before my heart starts banging in earnest. I take advantage of the howling wind to pant as audibly as I wish.

The ground is covered in layers of thick snow that yield to a second layer of volcanic ash. It looks like crumbled Oreo cookies and provides about as much resistance. There's the occasional flat rock to step on, which helps, but it's the low visibility that's stealing the show. I see no sign of this alleged second shelter. When I shout to Edgardo, asking him where the refuge is, I am told it's in a little place called "Tranquilo."

I can feel my heart pounding against polyester, trying to escape from my rib cage. I take my thumbs and lean them against the chest strap from the inside to relieve some of the pressure. *What has two thumbs and can't feel either of them? This gal!* Edgardo waits about thirty feet ahead of me with one foot up on a rock, as I huff and puff to shorten the distance between us. His befuddlement at my pace feels genuine. Pedro has been granted permission to go on without us. I can only imagine how that conversation went. *Just go, man. I'll deal with this bag of pasteur-ized milk bones.*

* * *

Turns out the reason I needed to conserve water is because there is no water in the refuge. Correction: there is water in a barrel by the toilets, but it's reserved for washing away feces. If we want drinking water, we will have to heat snow and then cool it. The irony here being that this is because one of the pipes is frozen.

On the ground floor of the refuge, there is a large space filled with booths that look exactly like the ski trip booths of my night-mares, as well as one inexplicably padlocked cabinet filled with bottles of Fiji water. Someone or someones had to do what I just did but while carting a giant glass door on their backs. They probably had to go back down for the padlock. Now it's taking about ten minutes to fill one pot and there are three burners for the fifteen people already here. And by people, I mean people with penises. Barring any surprises, I appear to be the only woman around. This is a coincidence. Just last night, a guide from Seattle tells me, there were two female climbers staying at the refuge.

What I can't understand is how he would possibly know this information. How long has he been here? Does he live here? If he lives here, should he not have figured out how to get into the goddamn cabinet by now?

It turns out he and his fellow climbers have been acclimatiz-ing at the refuge for two days. They have also ascended a couple of "minor mountains" in Peru in preparation for this one.

"That's funny," I say, even though it's not. "I got here last night."

"I thought you guys just arrived," the guide says, gesturing at Pedro.

He is untangling a pile of ropes across the room, a whole apple in his mouth.

"Nope." I am still watching Pedro. "I flew into Quito yesterday."

The guide's eyes widen. He asks if I'm on a medication called Diamox, which prevents altitude sickness by quickening the heart and thinning the blood. I am on no such medication. I have never even heard of it. I know that coca leaves are often chewed at Machu Picchu to prevent altitude sickness. I also know that Machu Picchu rests on a midget of a mountain, clocking in at under 8,000 feet. What should make me wary does make me wary. But despite my fear, it also fills me with pride. Preventive medication is for sissies. Me? I have the red blood cells of a goddamn Sherpa.

* * *

The idea of men traveling to push themselves to the limit is a culturally familiar one. Not every man hears the call of the wild, but those who do—the Krakauers and the Jungers—are not startled by the ringing. There is something inherently manly about climbing a mountain. Though, taken literally, that would make a deep-sea dive the most feminine activity on the planet. Perhaps it's less directly correlated to gender and more that mountaineering allows men to try on an idolized extension of their daily selves. Here is the prize for which a certain kind of man has been aiming with every beer chugged, every Super Bowl watched, every video game won, every drunken piggyback ride given to a one-hundred-pound girl. And now it's time to let the machismo run amok. You're on top of the world! Drink a shot of gasoline! Punch a bird! For women, to be on a mountain (assuming you're not a professional mountain climber) is not an extension of stereotypical behavior but a break from it. Therefore, to be part of a successful mountain-climbing expedition, it's important to play against the worst assumptions about one's own gender. Do this by being okay with more or less everything. Never refer to the pile of excrement on the outhouse floor as "icky." Try to avoid weeping when you feel your life may be in danger.

"I can't believe you're climbing this after one day," says a doctor from Baltimore, part of the Seattle hiker's team.

He translates for the third member of their party, a Chilean, who is so impressed he repeats it.

"*Un día!*"

At which point Edgardo, having just returned from the stove with a steaming pot of ramen noodles, gives the group a wave of his finger. He proceeds to rapidly debate with the doctor's Chilean friend.

"He says that this is not true." The doctor's translation has a five-second delay. "He says you have been in Quito for a week."

I grab his arm.

"Who said that?"

"Edgardo," says the doctor, eyes fixed on Edgardo's mouth as he speaks to me, "says you told him this."

Edgardo and I lock eyes. I look to him as a toddler looks at a parent, checking to see if this skinned knee is worth crying over. Should I flip out about this misunderstanding or not? But his face is inconclusive. He only shrugs optimistically. The doctor tries to comfort me. He explains that altitude sickness is unpredictable. There's nothing that says I'll definitely get it. Then again, there's nothing that says I won't.

I sit down and inhale as deeply as I can, which isn't very. The city of Quito, without even trying, is 9,000 feet above sea level. The friend who recommended I go see skeleton paintings is a playwright who came down with altitude sickness for eighteen hours upon landing. The friend who recommended I climb Cotopaxi did not. When I recount this story months later over a sea-level glass of wine, this second friend will remind me that he is a world traveler and Australian and that he *told* me climbing Cotopaxi was going to be "bloody hard."

"When we say something's hard, we mean it."

The question now is: Do I have theater geek lungs or Australian lungs?

"*Tranquilo*," Edgardo offers, putting his hand on my shoulder. "All will be fine."

I go outside into the crisp germ-free air and swallow a malaria pill with a fistful of snow. Up until now, my idea of coping with changes in atmospheric pressure was a nice big yawn. I look around at the fading outlines of the neighboring mountains. It's almost 7 p.m. I have five hours to mainline noodles and try to sleep before we head out. This I do in silence, coming back inside and sitting at a booth across from Edgardo and Pedro. There is nothing but the sound of wind and slurping.

* * *

Up a flight of narrow wooden stairs are a series of Holocaust beds. I wish there was a better means of describing them but rarely have I seen something that looks so much like something else. It's as if *The Brady Bunch* were filmed in Nazi Germany and we're spending the night on set. There's a flurry of multilingual whisper-shouting as climbing partners bid each other good night in the semidarkness. I heave my backpack onto the top of an unoccupied bunk and it bounces on the mattress.

"I sleep downstairs," says Edgardo, who will never explain why this is, "but I keep my pack here."

"Sounds fine," I say, fiddling with the zippers on my backpack.

I'm not mad at him, not really. My predicament could have been easily avoided with some minimal research on my part. I know that one day I will be relieved that I had not seen a photograph of Cotopaxi prior to being located on it. Because if I had, I never would have come. One day I will try to remember but ultimately forget feeling as sick as I'm about to feel. I'll just think: Here is something I did. But right now, looking at the clusters of confident climbers around me, I feel like I got saddled with the worst lab partner in the world.

Of the myriad garbled mutterings that spew forth from Edgardo's mouth, it is unfortunate that his paranoia about crime is not one of them. He knows how to say "Watch your shit" in English as well as he does in Spanish. I can feel us being overheard as my bunkmates climb into their squeaky beds. I can sense them bristle in the dark, as they've nothing better to do than listen to our conversation. I worry that by sheer association with Edgardo, I will be the victim of punitive theft or molestation. The latter of which would be welcome so long as the molesting process consists of a vigorous foot rubbing.

"Keep all of your eyes on my stuff," Edgardo practically shouts.

He gestures at my borrowed backpack, which also happens to have his new climbing helmet strapped to it. Go to sleep but also watch his stuff? Sleep with one eye open? That's more of an expression than a possibility.

"And what is this?" He points at my bunk.

"What is what?"

I can't imagine to what he's referring. The bare mattress you'd cross the street to avoid if you saw it in New York? But then he plucks a small leather case from my bed. Along with my dwindling bottle of water and sleeping bag, that's all I have on me.

"You have too many things," he says, gesturing at my series of invisible steamer trunks. "We need to go light." He rattles the leather case in my face. "You need this?"

"Yes." I grab it back. "I do."

"It goes in the backpack."

"I don't think so."

"Why?"

Everyone in the room not magically asleep by 7 p.m. is hushed and listening, waiting for the squall to pass.

"Fine," I hiss. "You want to do this? Let's do this."

I mumble under my breath as I open the case. My thumbs are numb. There has to be as much of a male aversion to open discussion of feminine hygiene on this continent as there is on mine. I hold up three tampons, fanning them out like cards. Or scissors.

Scissors for hands. Edgardo squints at them, momentarily confounded by the foreign packaging. Recognition sets in.

"Okay, okay," he says.

"Okay?" I snap.

Great. Now I've completely blown my chances at molestation. A Frenchman on the bunk next to mine starts snickering and Edgardo glares at him. The Frenchman rolls over in his sleeping bag, where he whispers to his partner on the other side. At one point in the night I shake so uncontrollably, I climb down to the ground and move my whole bunk a few inches away so as not to put his bed on vibrate.

* * *

The following cannot be overstated: Had I known what I was getting into, the thing I would have left home with—my emotional EpiPen—is a friend. Someone I trusted. Someone I had slept with. Someone who already knew my name. Someone to whom I owed money and who thus had a vested interest in seeing me make it off Cotopaxi in one piece. All the mountain-climbing accounts I have read post-Cotopaxi seem to say the same thing: You'd be an idiot to climb a major mountain alone. More than experiencing dehydration as your feet punch through the very substance that might otherwise hydrate you, loneliness is one of the elements. And no mountain guide in the world, good or bad, can protect you from that.

There is a rip in Pedro's sleeping bag. As the night ticks on, I want to spread the extra fleece jacket lent to me by the Seattle guide over my already layered body, maybe stick my hands in the sleeve ends. But every time I move to retrieve the fleece, the sleeping bag rips a little more. The rip is cunning, a worthy adversary. It will not be tricked by me slowly lifting my knees or gradually extending an arm down from the side.

Frustrated, dizzy, and desperate to get to the outhouse, finally I just sit up. The rip shows no mercy and now runs the full length of the sleeping bag. When I return, I have to clamp it shut between my knees. I experiment with comfort, using my forearm as a pillow. But the skin exposed by being forced out of the sleeping bag gets cold too quickly. It's unacceptable for my hands to be anywhere but my armpits or between my legs. I think of the expression "chilled to the bone" and wonder what comes after that. Chilled to the marrow? Then what? If you hit the center of the center of the center, do you just start blowing icicles out your nose? I think again of my apartment in July. My goal is to convince myself that it's too hot for sleep, that I have just kicked the comforter to the ground and a simple sheet is oppressive to my skin. I strain to hear the sound of that summer rain falling on metal.

If a beetle could survive up here, I would see its breath.

Around 3 a.m., I sit up in a panic, clutching my throat. I had started drifting off. This would have been a good thing if I wasn't also displaying the first signs of altitude sickness. Anyone who has ever been awake and then gone to sleep is familiar with the concept of slowed breathing. But if you're already struggling to breathe, slipping into slumber feels like an invisible force is trying to choke the life out of you. I look around me at the occupied mattresses and sigh in a pitiable fashion. I'm dehydrated and losing iron to a little cotton finger between my legs. I touch my forehead, disturbed by how good it feels to have this abnormally cold part of my body comfort this abnormally hot part of my body. I lie awake, wheeze, and wait, watching Edgardo's new helmet not move on the floor below. I wonder again about the weight of inexperience. What percentage of this is my fault? How much of this is my ignorance and how much of it is the mountain's difficulty? It feels like guessing beans in a jar.

Just before midnight a dainty chorus of digital watch alarms commences. Headlamps are flicked on as, one by one, climbers yawn in various languages. Now, a normal person—and I like to include myself in this category whenever possible—might have stayed in bed at this juncture. Especially with some ilk of ailment that feels akin to going on a carousel with a hangover. But I am here and I can't not be here. Climbing and not climbing somehow feel like the same thing.

As I come downstairs, I clutch a railing with one hand and an "I'm still drunk and might throw up on the subway" plastic bag in the other. I see that the doctor and his expedition have already gone. Climbers gear up around me, talking about how the conditions have been iffy. There's a storm that could get worse. Some people are concerned about a particularly avalanche-prone bend in the terrain. Unfortunately, I don't have the mental palate to discern what "iffy" means. Not until we start our ascent.

This climb is not terribly different from yesterday's, save for the fact that it's pitch-black. At first everything is still, the mountain equivalent of a man-made lake at night. But soon the wind starts coming after us and brings with it an especially overpowering brand of sleet. I don't so much feel like I'm on the movie set of a snowstorm as on the movie set of a snowstorm that's being blown away by an actual snowstorm. Over the icy ground and into the dark, the other groups move ahead. Pedro and Edgardo are forced to wait for me. I move slower than a Galápagos turtle and am generally a total drag.

"Come on!" shouts Edgardo.

"I'm honestly going to kill you!" I shout back, adding a sing-songy "Fuck your mother" for my own benefit.

To keep myself going, I count to five as I step, then start over. Also of assistance is following the spotlight of my headlamp as it points down. I start counting the bounces of light as I plunge one foot in front of the other. I am, I believe, just above 16,000 feet above sea level. To be clear, around 17,000 feet is the height at which you're liable to believe your companion is an orange and attempt to peel him.

Still, I press on, thinking I will be able to outsmart such delusions. You see, We, the People of Sea Level, have a tough time believing in externally induced insanity. You say you're born with the sociopathic strain that compels you to burn ants with a magnifying glass? Sure, fine, whatever. Be crazy. But if you are not this person, if you are more or less regular, we will spend the rest of your life teaching you to believe in the power of your mind over the matter of your body. This belief is vital to our existence. We use it for dieting and productivity and heartbreak and exhaustion. Physical pain is the body's retort to such hubris. Control was an illusion. You were having a lucid dream, my friend. What the mind really is, is a Tupperware container full of leftover noodles.

* * *

I once sat next to a man on a plane who had climbed Everest and thus had stood approximately 900 feet below the level of our seats. He went with his wife, a champion mountain climber famous in Eastern Europe, as well as several professional guides. They were equipped with all the tents and oxygen tanks money could buy. Still, one never knows how one will react in an environment about as hospitable to humans as the bottom of the ocean. I imagine this is part of the thrill of mountain climbing if you are remotely experienced and already 90 percent sure of how you'll respond to specific conditions. The rest is a reasonable margin for the un-known. This man's wife had a bronchial infection within that mar-gin. One thing led to another, which led to her almost choking to death on a piece of her own lung. She turned blue and had to be carried to a tent where one of the guides felt her pulse and mistak-enly pronounced her dead. The man was confused.

"I said, 'What do you mean, my wife is dead?' and the guide said, 'She's not breathing.'"

"And then what did you *do*?" I asked, enraptured.

This man and I had bonded over a hostile flight attendant when we boarded. For the next few hours, he was as good as family. I leaned on our shared armrest and put my chin in my palm.

"I said . . . 'Okay.'"

"What? That's it?!"

He explained that the unholy trinity of exhaustion, cold, and reduced oxygen can lead to extreme calm. It's not that you can't think straight, it's that you can *only* think straight. There is no emotion, just a slow and methodical logic mirroring the crunch of your steps. One foot in front of the other. The man's wife was not breathing, which meant she must be dead and he wanted to know what came next. Still, I knew some part of him must have been devastated at the idea of losing his wife. He considered this.

"I might have also said, 'That's not good.'"

As for Cotopaxi, it is only like Everest in that it's got snow on it. And it's higher than wherever you are right now, unless you're reading this on an airplane. Climbing Cotopaxi is something that gets done daily, whereas about 5,000 people total have summited Everest. With the possible exception of watching an *Inside the Actors Studio* marathon, conquering Everest is the most difficult thing a human being can do. And yet as I push forward in the dark, I imagine a colossal 747 airplane swinging by to pick me up where I stand. It slows down just long enough for me to lasso my climbing rope over the wing and takes me somewhere with mugs of hot chocolate.

At the next bend, one of the headlights ahead of me pauses and shines backward in my direction. It waits for the distance between us to close. Edgardo's ponytail is covered in snow. It looks gray.

"Okay?" he asks, meaning "If the answer's not 'yes,' I wash my hands of you."

I say nothing for a second, struggling to breathe. I don't like going for a light jog and chatting at the same time. I lean on my knees and wheeze.

"I think my legs are bigger than my lungs," I say.

"I don't understand this," he says.

Neither do I, I think. My unacclimatized ass lasts approximately twenty more minutes in the dark before huddling over at 17,500 feet. I make the volcano an offering of partially digested beans. I am not the first to puke on this glacier and I won't be the last. I can taste the bitterness of the malaria pill.

One's instinct, when depending on something faulty, is to immediately stop depending on that thing. It only takes a moment of balancing a refrigerator on stilts to realize it's time to put the refrigerator elsewhere. But to have there be no "elsewhere," to have your body betray you, is a frightening sensation. You want an extra heart to help this one pump blood. But there is no extra heart. It's like going through a breakup and wanting to talk about your distress with the person who just dumped you.

I wipe my face with snow and tilt my head back. Between gusts of white is a deep black sky. Imposing ice formations rise like monuments in the distance. Cotopaxi's crater will have to be stunning for everyone but me.

I am done here.

With Pedro in tow, Edgardo and I make our way down the mountain. My fevered brain finds the language barrier disproportionately comical and every time Edgardo shouts at me over the wind, I have to sit down and laugh until I can't breathe. This only irritates him more. Back at the refuge, I request that he rifle through the Baltimore doctor's things for a thermometer. He looks appalled. Edgardo sincerely thinks I'd like to steal from my bunkmates. Yes, that's right. There's a thermometer shortage so grave in the United States, the government had me fly to Ecuador and fake altitude sickness so that I might do an undercover sweep for medical supplies. Though, to Edgardo's credit, neither of us is a genius at this hour. Had we had our heads screwed on straight, it might have occurred to one of us to crack open the first-aid kit buried in the bottom of his backpack this entire time.

The chances of my having a fever are high, much like the fever it turns out I have. I know this because around 3 a.m., I ask Pedro why so many people are back already. He doesn't understand what I mean.

"The headlights," I whisper, gesturing at the wall across from my bunk, where tiny spotlights bounce on the wood.

Pedro shakes his head. I think he's a moron. He thinks I'm a moron.

"People coming up the stairs," I stress.

"No light," he whispers.

Although the conditions were bad enough to cut short the summit goal for many, a fact that will make me feel like less of a wimp even as I have sworn off testosterone-fueled notions of achievement, I was the one who broke first. No one else will return for another hour.

"Oh, good," I say, rolling over. "That's perfect."

I am lucid enough to be disappointed by my own insanity.

* * *

Among the defeated is the French hiker who gets down from his bunk no sooner than he catches his breath. He talks to me, telling me the occasional joke that makes me cough and muster a *"Oui, c'est drôle. C'est très drôle."* He holds my shivering hand for an hour straight. It's long enough for me to think that not only is this the kindest thing anyone has ever done for me but also the kindest thing I have ever personally witnessed someone do for a stranger. Eventually the Seattle hiker marches up to me and asks to pull my finger. From the top bunk, I see all of these people as floating heads, amateur doctors making their rounds.

"Let me see her finger," he says to the others.

This is no time for third-grade games, sir.

He clips a heartbeat monitor to my thumb.

My heart rate is less than enthusiastic.

What has two thumbs and no pulse? This girl!

"Hmmm," he says.

They watch as I slide the monitor from my thumb in slow motion. It snaps back together and falls to the floor. I don't remember anyone touching my forehead but a voice announces that I'm burning up. I push myself upright.

"Okay," I say, "what are the worst times to go down?"

Pedro lifts the top layer of his sleeping bag.

"Hey!" he says. "There's a rip in this!"

"Probably between five and seven," says the Seattle climber, pressing his watch to make it glow.

It's 5 a.m. In daylight, it would take me forty minutes to get down from the refuge. In my current condition, I suspect it will take me longer than that to get down from this bunk. I decide to wait it out, which entails more nausea and an irrepressible chill. Still, it's not like I'm dying. At least that's what I tell my French friend when he asks me if I'm dying. I have never been asked this in a sincere fashion before. I am flattered that he thinks I would know. People who regularly push themselves to the brink of their physical limitations know what dying feels like. When I say something tastes like pennies or piss or shit, I'm not implying a frame of reference for these flavors. But these people—they eat shit for fun.

* * *

The mountain pretends not to know what it did. At sunrise, it looks perfectly innocent, as if it has just chewed my shoe and now it wants to go for a walk. Fever broken, standing outside in the quiet, I wait for Edgardo and Pedro to wake up. The refuge is perched on a ledge so that the view runs right up to my feet. Twin rainbows appear in the valleys in front of me. The contrast of green hills and snowcapped tops gives the entire region a confectionary look. The mountains themselves look like humpback whales coming up for air. It's all so offensively pretty. There's not a sign of last night's storm. You could put a feather on top of the snow and it wouldn't blow away. For a split second, I kick myself for not having climbed higher last night. This, I think, is how abusive relationships get their start.

I hear a crunch on the ground behind me.

"Imbabura," Edgardo announces, pointing to my right.

There, surrounded by mist, is the mountain I didn't climb. It's the least snowcapped of the mountains. Snow yarmulked.

I nod. "It's beautiful."

"I take this," Edgardo says as he grabs my backpack for me.

"Thank you," I say, and mean it.

I am relieved to not compound the thumping in my skull by climbing down with the extra weight. Edgardo unfastens his new helmet and clips it to his own bag. Then he hands the pack back to me. When I don't immediately take it, he ever so gently rests it against my leg.

"*De nada,*" he says, smiling.

* * *

When we arrive at the car, I am somehow surprised to see it there, right where we parked it. Unlike Edgardo, I did not expect it to get stolen. But I am surprised to see it so unaffected by last night's events. By the time I reach for the door handle, my body is almost back to normal, as indifferent to Cotopaxi as the car is.

Edgardo's foot is heavy on the gas pedal. I would sooner drink a bottle of whiskey and run down a spiral staircase than drive around with Edgardo again. But as I have neither at my disposal, I buckle up.

"Look," Edgardo says, once we are at the base of the mountain.

"What?"

He ignores me and stops the car. At first I see nothing. Then, on the hillside, meandering between shrubs, are five spots. They're moving slowly toward us. They are wild horses, four caramel and one black. As they get closer, I see their manes are tangled with unknowable debris. Some of their ribs show when they move. Edgardo grabs his camera from the backseat and gets out of the car to take pictures. He moves with theatrical stealth, trying not to frighten them. They remain calm, stopping to munch on long grass while keeping one eye on Edgardo. This is what he needed last night, an animal with monocular vision to watch his shit.

Our driver missing, Pedro and I get out of the Jeep, closing our doors softly behind us. We lean together, watching Edgardo creep up on the horses, trying to crouch down and move forward at the same time. The sun is bright, my breathing regular. I have done the unthinkable: unzipped my jacket. Pedro laughs at his friend under his breath and shakes his head. He takes papers out of his pocket, sprinkles some dried leaves inside and rolls a joint, expertly sealing it with his tongue. He lights it and hands it to me. As I inhale, Pedro cleans his Oakleys with his shirt, glares at the sky, and says we have to get going. It's going to rain again. The road to the highway will be covered in mud. He removes a knife and a mango from his other pocket, cuts the mango, and eats chunks directly from the blade.

"He is heartsick," explains Pedro, placing the knife against his chest, concerned he got the expression wrong.

He gestures at Edgardo with the knife.

"There is a woman he loves and she will not call him. So he texts her. A lot."

The idea of Edgardo living his life, drinking, texting, going to techno nights at clubs and flirtatiously moving his ponytail down women's faces like a paintbrush, is amusing to me.

"He lives with his mother," Pedro continues, "but he wants to move with this woman."

"Does she ever respond to the texts?"

"She has a new boyfriend. Edgardo knows a little but he doesn't really know."

From half a football field away, the wind carries the sound of Edgardo telling the horses to be "*tranquilo*," which they already are. They're not running from him nor are they charging him. They're just casually meandering away.

"Do you know this guy?"

"He is my brother."

"I see," I say with a my-wife-is-dead level of energy. "That's not good."

"No." Pedro laughs. "It's not."

He offers me the mango, which I take in exchange for the second half of the joint.

When Edgardo comes back to the car, I stare out the window, refusing to feel bad for him. I will not care who broke Edgardo's heart or why or how badly. I am not sorry he is lonely. A lot of people are lonely. A lot of people are lonely even when they're surrounded by other people. I am determined to deny him my empathy. But everything is thawing, inside the car and out. So when Edgardo enthusiastically shouts the names of the mountains, releasing the steering wheel to point each time the road provides a new angle, as if I have not just spent the night on one of them, as if he has not told me a million times already, I can't help but crane my neck and nod, sufficiently awed.

The
Grape
Man

MY ROOMMATE CAME RUNNING OUT OF THE CLOSET AND DID NOT stop until he reached Los Angeles. I knew this day would come. Sometimes it's easier to be your actual self where nothing of your alleged self exists. Sometimes that's how you find out who you are in the first place. But after three years of cohabitation, I knew I would never find a better roommate than him, decoratively, hygienically, or morally. The day my previous roommate moved out, he caught her and a friend escorting her queen-size mattress up to the tar roof of our building, where they intended to discard it. The apartment was on the fifth floor of a fifth-floor walk-up, so it was easier to battle gravity for one flight than pivot down a narrow stairwell for four. He stopped her, saying something like, "Hey, that's not where that goes." I wouldn't have. I would have tattled or seethed or judged or indulged in all three at once, like dipping sauces.

Instead of rolling the dice with another roommate, I decided it was finally time to live on my own. So I moved to a studio apartment on the first floor of an old brownstone, right above the garden unit. What used to be an Edith Wharton character's yarn storage room was now my entire world. The cliché about New York starter apartments is that the shower is in the kitchen. The good news is this joke didn't apply to me. The bad news is this is because there was no shower, only a bathtub.

Still, the place had whimsical touches. Like an outlet on the upper right-hand corner of one of the walls that suggested the building had once been upside down. Or the radiator that someone had taken the liberty of spray-painting gold. Or the defunct buzzer on the door frame that had once been used to ring for a maid. Now it was frozen beneath layers of white paint, its cords clipped. I didn't need to ring for a maid, anyway. I was my own maid. I used to scrub down the whole place in ten minutes, using paper towels and Windex, cleaning the windows to get a better view of the greenery below.

Most people I knew who were lucky enough to have outdoor space used it for damp parties strung from above with Chinese lanterns or as a necropolis for broken patio furniture. The garden apartment was a thing to be trampled on or, when the situation called for it, puked near. Whatever weeds pushed themselves between seams in the concrete constituted "the garden." But not this garden. Here I was, living above Don, a sixty-something man with a NO NUKES sticker on his door and a deeply green thumb. Don meticulously kept a wall-to-wall garden of flowers and topiaries, of vegetable trellises and canopies of vines. It was extraordinary. To this day, it is the only one of its kind I've seen.

I never knew Don's last name. Or rather, I did on the day I moved in and he shook my hand with a calloused paw, but I have long since forgotten it. What I do know is that he was the thing rarer than a baby-pigeon sighting in New York—a neighbor with whom you enjoy interacting. After his name, the second piece of information Don offered pertained to his grapevines, which were at their peak. If the vines got too unruly, I should let him know. They were Champagne grapes, he explained, small, dark, and seedless. I didn't think much of this warning at the time. My previous bedroom window had faced a brick wall—how unsightly could a bunch of grapevines be? And who was I to spit in Mother Nature's bucolic face? I also figured he was overplaying his gardening skills. I lived a full floor above him. Those would have to be some pretty determined vines to climb so far and so fast.

Within a few weeks, they had completely obstructed the bathroom and living room windows. Which was all the windows. It was like living in an organic jail cell. The vines moved at a grape-specific speed, somewhere between stop-motion animation and full-blown horror movie. At first their tendrils cast playful shadows on my walls, but now they were like Michael Pollan's wet dream run amok. When I lifted the windowpane to get some fresh air, branches flopped inward and onto my radiator, unbending as if they had eaten too much and had just now been permitted to unbutton their pants. And my apartment was but a pit stop for them as they made their way to the window above mine.

On the plus side? What an olden-timey way to discourage bur-
glars! Cheaper than an alligator moat. On the minus side? Off-
Seasonal Affective Disorder.

If I had been my old roommate, I would have said something.
He lived and died by Occam's razor, whereas I seemed to be in
the midst of a multidecade phase of making everything more
complicated than it needed to be. Here I was, unambiguously
invited to say something if I saw something. Instead, I decided to
resolve the situation myself. Not wanting to make Don get out his
industrial ladder and climb up to my window in threadbare boxer
shorts, I would reach out every few days with a pair of kitchen scissors. But no matter how deep into the V of the scissors I crammed
the vines, they only slid back out. I barely nicked them. Come July,
I had to use a cleaver. Which also meant I had to buy a cleaver.
But every woman should own a cleaver.

And it worked. The mosses and flowers and a softly bubbling
fountain came into view. There was a roughly cut stone path of
the Zen persuasion. It was lovely. For a whole seventy-two hours.
Until it wasn't again.

One day Don stopped me as I was coming out of our local
Laundromat. He was wearing a striped caftan and green rain boots
with plastic amphibian eyes molded to the toes. He had taken
notice of the attempted trimming. He told me that he would
have done the pruning himself and seemed borderline offended
that I had taken this task off his hands. I hadn't realized it was a
betrayal of our neighborly relations and, in fact, assumed that
Don of all people would appreciate communal gardening. He
blew a lock of white hair from his forehead and added that he
hoped I at least ate the grapes because he didn't know what else

to do with them. He had only one family member in New York, a ninety-seven-year-old mother in a nursing home with "no appetite and no charisma," and the rest of his friends were back in Portland, Oregon, having swapped opiates and Airstreams for lattes and refurbished Airstreams. He made me promise to eat some of the grapes. Then he insisted on carrying my laundry as we walked home.

At first, I was resistant. Eat the grapes? Eat them? Grapes that had come from city soil and rested on the same brick wall from which my air conditioner protruded? Oh, no, thank you. But both the grapes and the promise I had made dangled themselves before me. So one day I reached out the window and tore off a couple of ripe helixes. I soaked them in my sink. Then I put them in the refrigerator. If I couldn't kill the germs, I could at least make them wish they were dead.

The highest compliment bestowed upon fruit is that it tastes "like candy." Pineapple gets this a lot. Raspberries. Star fruit's certainly sick of hearing it. What's meant to be a compliment to fruit is actually an insult to candy. I don't know what kind of Eastern-bloc chalk pellets people have been eating, but most grapes do not taste as awesome as candy. Except for these. These were like little clown cars of sugar and flavor. And they were accessible from my bathtub, where I could reach my arm out, snap off a cluster, and knock my head back like a Greek goddess.

To thank Don, I hung a bottle of red wine in a paper bag around his doorknob, along with a note that I'm sorry to report included the phrase "grapes of bath." Before long, we became engaged in a game of Obvious Santa. Don really amped things up. In return for the wine, he left me a bag of freshly picked tomatoes tied with red ribbons. In return for the tomatoes, I left him a beer koozie with dancing rainbow bears printed on the side. He left me a flower vase. I left him flower food. He left me a bottle of organic laundry detergent. I left him hand balm. He left me a yoga mat. I left him the same yoga mat with a package of Hostess cupcakes tied to it.

After about a month of this, I returned home from work one day to find an actual present wrapped in paper and ribbon, waiting for me outside my door.

I'm guessing you could use this, read the attached note.

Inside was a glossy photo book called *Designing with Books*. I was still working in book publishing and Don had registered the rectangular packages I received. It was the first gift that didn't seem spontaneous, that hadn't impulsively occurred to either of us. He had tracked it down especially for me. So at the office the next day, I did some digging of my own. Turns out I worked for the same people who produced such sleeper hits as *Gardening in Small Spaces*. Presumably this series also includes *Reading on Stools* and *Napping Under Partial Enclosures*. I ordered a copy of *Gardening in Small Spaces* and left it outside Don's door, along with a trowel. He was the only person I knew who could use it without hitting concrete.

* * *

The other thing that made Don so great is that he was considerate without being intrusive—unlike our super, who was a professional lunatic. This man terrorized our building, inventing minor crimes for which anyone could be tried. Offenses included: being too rough with the front door, tracking dirt into the basement, standing outside while talking on the phone, allowing vagrants (food delivery people) to enter the building, and hosting scumbags (friends) and degenerates (members of the opposite sex). All of whom demonstrated reckless behavior. Like opening the front door.

If your toilet clogged, he gave you the side-eye. If your ceiling caved in, he yelled at you for having a ceiling. Once, he banged on my door at 7 a.m., and when I opened it, bathrobed and bleary-eyed, he accused me of letting my packages languish on the lobby radiator. I explained to him that not only was this false, but it could never be true. I was living on my own for the first time. I took no vacations. I wrote on weekends. A package was confirmation of my existence. The mailman himself didn't monitor package delivery as I did. Also, *lobby* was an ambitious term for it.

"Then how do you explain this?!" he shouted.

At his feet was a box stained from the inside. It smelled of melted chocolate. On the side of the box was stamped: THE LAST STRAW(BERRIES)!™

Even if I had associated with the kind of people who might tar and feather berries and ship them to me, this seemed like more of a 3 p.m. issue. I crouched down and examined the box, which was addressed to 1F. Which was not my apartment number. It was Don's.

"Oh," our super said, storming off with the box under his arm.

Don, too, had the mayoral streak that comes with twenty years of living in the same building, but he smoked too much weed to get wound up about it. The notes Don taped to the front door were upbeat scribbles about what not to do with one's plastic bottles and what to do when closing the front door. *Be gentle!*

Leave this world better than you found it! Peace & love, Don. I overheard him doling out lectures to new tenants about newspaper stealing that were so heartfelt, I felt guilty. Even when it was my paper that was getting stolen. He left sandwiches for the crack addict who sometimes slept in our vestibule with her knees tucked into her T-shirt, the scent of her lack of other habits seeping into the hallway and under my apartment door. Rolling a towel beneath my door became part of my nightly ritual. I suspected it was part of Don's, too, though for a different reason.

So inspired was I by Don's hempish embrace of the world, I salvaged a wobbly end table from the street, drowned it in disinfectant, and put it in the hall outside my door. I also put a disposable glass vase on it, which Don took to filling with flowers. With a fluorescent hallway bulb as their only light source, the flowers were doomed to perish at an epidemic rate. And yet Don replaced them regularly and without fanfare. When he got wind that I'd be publishing a book of my own, he seemed legitimately concerned that I would be made uncomfortable by the flowers.

"In what way would flowers make me uncomfortable?"

"Well, now that you're famous," he explained, "you'll probably get creepy things all the time."

I tried to imagine the world, now gone, from which Don hailed—a pre-Internet world in which there was only one brand of fame and you either were or you weren't.

"That's not how book publishing works," I told him.

In truth, I had already received a piece of fan mail. It was in the form of a VHS tape from a hoarder in Boise who had read an excerpt of my book. The tape featured an hour of this guy speaking to the camera in front of a backdrop of board games and piles of Tupperware containing foods in competing states of decay. He talked about his gig as an SAT tutor while some birds chirped in a cage off camera. He was sane and harmless in the way that people who have grown to expect little from the world are sane and harmless. To this day, I'm not sure how he got my address but I choose to remain unconcerned about it. For one thing, I don't live there anymore. For another, who am I to hoarder-shame anyone when I'm the one with the VHS player?

* * *

One night, after a bad day at work, I returned home to find a single iris resting on the building's stoop. It was big and floppy, plucked up by the root. I spotted it from down the block. I couldn't understand why the flower was outside and alone instead of in the vase and in the company of other flowers. But I had a hunch as to who had put it there. I twirled the stem between my fingers, glancing down at the note that had been left underneath.

Written in unfamiliar ballpoint, it read: *To our beloved neighbor Don of many years . . . you will be missed.*

I dropped my bag and sat on my stoop, where I reread the note several times. I felt that shameful charge in the nerves that occurs when something big happens. Before your brain has a chance to parse if it's good big or bad big, the information goes into a kind of processing center for all eventful things. I wanted to cry, but I had wanted to cry before the introduction of the flower. It felt cheap to cull the emotion from one less-than-ideal day in order to have the ideal response to Don's death.

You will be missed.

Proportionally, I hadn't known Don well enough to burst into tears—but I also hadn't known him little enough to go inside like nothing had happened. I called my old roommate in LA. I was unsure of where to put this tragedy that was not entirely mine. I wanted to drag it up to the roof of emotionally miscellaneous occurrences and leave it there.

"Well, that's the thing about New York," he said.

"There are a lot of 'things' about New York," I groaned.

"True," he conceded. "Except for death. Death is New York–specific."

I balked at this. Death is not a regionally specific experience. It comes for us all. Death and taxes. Actually, just death. The Cayman Islands don't have taxes.

"I mean the way New Yorkers *handle* death," he clarified. "They don't know how to mourn for people they only sort of know. It's too abstract for such an opinionated culture. That's why 9/11 was such a mess."

"Oh, is that why?"

"I gotta go," he said. "I'm going to a party in Venice."

"Fine," I said. "I hope you get trapped in traffic forever."

I picked up the flower and took a big sniff. Alas, as Don could have told me, irises don't smell like anything.

* * *

By the next morning, more flowers had appeared on the stoop and someone had drawn a sad face on the original note. There was also a bag of almonds and a squeegee, signs of other friends in the building, of other private jokes that were now one-way. These objects provided me with a sense of comfort when I bumped into my super, his gruffness barely pruned by death. He told me that Don made a wrong turn on his motorcycle, drove headlong into a bus on Second Avenue, and was in a coma for six days before he died. My super seemed surprised by my upset.

"He sent those berries to himself, you know."

I think part of me had known that. I never heard a single visitor in Don's apartment. I never ran into him on the street accompanied by anyone but himself. I never saw him with more than one bag of groceries in his hand. To live alone can be a glorious thing. Between jags of crippling loneliness and wretched TV, it's an education in self-sufficiency, self-actualization, and self-tanner. But it is possible to have too many rooms of one's own.

There was a service for Don at an Italian restaurant in Jersey City. I didn't know he had family in Jersey City. I also didn't go. The invitation asked for charitable donations instead of flowers. I sent neither, though I knew Don would have liked both. But perhaps that's tribute enough, having people around who knew that you were here, who can say what you would have liked. I tried to keep up Don's habit of putting flowers in the vase. But my flowers were half as nice and twice as expensive. You really have to buy two bunches of the bodega kind unless you want your vase to look more wretched than it did before you put the flowers in. I also did not enjoy the face the bodega man made each time I told him that he didn't have to bother wrapping my roses in paper.

The new tenants moved in quickly. These neighbors were also adults but a different brand of adult than Don. They wanted a place to sit outside and read the Sunday paper, a place for their toddler to play that wasn't a coliseum of thorns and jagged rocks. They wanted patio furniture with cushions and they got it. They uprooted everything, including the vegetables and the moss, including the grapevines. I had to install curtains.

Right
Aid

AT MY LOCAL RITE AID WORKS A WOMAN WHO ONCE LOOKED AT MY ID and said, "We have the same birthday!" She hasn't mentioned it since. I think how I might like to surprise her with this information on the day. But that will mean both that I am in a Rite Aid on my birthday and that I am still smoking cigarettes. Instead, I go in a few days before our big day, in need of paper towels. I ask her if she has any exciting weekend plans. She blinks at me, processing the question. Then she tells me that she only dates men.

Relative
Stranger

THE MOST IMPORTANT THING YOU NEED TO KNOW ABOUT MY uncle, the porn star, is that he's not my actual uncle. He's my mother's cousin, which makes him my first cousin once removed. The oldest of three brothers, Johnny is now a seventy-four-year-old man partial to books-on-tape and cantaloupe, but between 1973 and 1987, he starred in 116 adult films. He was Man in Car, Man with Book, Man on Bus, Man in Hot Tub, Orgy Guy in Red Chair, Party Guy, Guy Wearing Glasses, Delivery Boy, and, perplexingly, Guy in Credits. He was the porn equivalent of Barbie, who can count astronaut, zookeeper, and aerobics instructor among her professional accomplishments. Except that Barbie, like Jesus before her and Prince after her, has no last name. Whereas Johnny's last name, his actual last name, is Seeman. This is a fact too absurd to warrant further analysis.

I didn't snoop around about Johnny until college, but this was not for lack of interest. My college years happened to coincide with the late nineties, when the Internet was fast becoming a tool for personal research. Before that, my generation mostly used it for chain letters and lightbulb jokes—*How many Harvard students does it take to change a lightbulb? Two. One to hold the lightbulb and the other to rotate the world around him.* But suddenly I had a vehicle for my curiosity. So I looked up Johnny to see what I could find. I was neither brave nor willing enough to search for video footage for fear of noticing any genetic resemblance to my mother's brothers. Even the Greeks don't have a name for that specific a complex. Instead, I read. My favorite article to this day was one in which Johnny is referred to—revered by, really—as the most famous stunt cock ever. That was the headline—*Johnny Seeman: The Most Famous Stunt Cock Ever.*

This superlative seared into my brain. How many self-identifying stunt cocks have walked the earth to make "ever" meaningful? Forty? "Ever" seemed a touch hyperbolic for an unquantifiable group of people. I also wondered if Johnny's unique endowments meant I, too, had the good genitalia gene. If I have a son, will he be pretty much set in that department? That might be a nice bonus attribute, though hopefully not one he will have to rely on for money.

In case you're not familiar, a stunt cock is the guy who steps in to produce the money shot if an actor can't maintain an erection. I imagine this was handy in the era before little blue pills and digital film, but it seems like a real morale dampener for everyone else. This is the guy who opens the pickle jar after you've loosened it, the one who carries the birthday cake you baked out of the kitchen. More than anything, it struck me as an odd hook for an interview. It's the kind of detail that a man might drop about himself, but would be less likely to point out about another man. Unless, of course, it was the sole reason for an article that might not exist otherwise. And there, if you will, was the rub. I got the sense that, despite his 116 films, Johnny had been all but forgotten. In pornography, being tag-teamed by three women and a vacuum cleaner nozzle does not a legend make. Johnny needed to be reintroduced.

* * *

Like I said, the man's not my uncle. Though I've known Johnny my whole life, I can count our interactions on one hand. Our family is not the reunion type. We're either united already or distant for some very good reason. Growing up, I saw Johnny at funerals and shivas, possibly a wedding—definitely one Thanksgiving when my father got a real kick out of offering him breast meat. And yet we referred to him as "uncle" in a way we did not with his brothers, who were cast as childhood friends of my mother's.

A combination of factors made this possible. For starters, my otherwise straitlaced parents could barely contain their excitement at having a porn star in their midst. A porn star is chum in the water for people who think getting wait-listed from college is a haunting secret. Also, Johnny's other brothers are both doctors. One practices in Paris, which means he can say things like "femur" in French (*fémur*). Even I will concede this is a dramatic divergence in life paths—it's not as if the other brothers work in marketing or club promotion. But my parents' reverse mythologizing of Johnny made it impossible to get an accurate sense of the guy. Which is my family's way.

One of their favorite pastimes is diagnosing a person's entire character by latching on to arbitrary details. They're really good at it. When I was twelve, my friend Alexis and I were watching TV in my parents' bedroom. Alexis was lying on the bed with her chin in her palms when my mother entered the room. Alexis said hello, but failed to remove her feet from where they rested—on my mother's pillow. And that was that. I tried to defend my friend, citing the layer of sock that separated her feet from where my mother put her face, but it was no use. When Alexis and I had a falling-out years later, my mother danced on the grave of the friendship.

"That girl," she reiterated, "was a bad influence."

Meanwhile, my friend Dave, who once tried convincing me to have sex in the back of a van so we could "knock it out" before college, could do no wrong after once ringing the doorbell with our newspaper in hand.

In this same way, snippets about Johnny were presented as essentials or in lieu of essentials. I knew that he dropped out of UNC Chapel Hill, which meant he was smart enough to get in, and that he'd spent the last thirty years living alone in an apartment somewhere in Los Angeles, which meant he was sad. I knew he was once so lost to a world of sex-crazed degenerates that he sent his mother, my great-aunt, a magazine with an advertisement for one of his films. The photo featured Johnny, bespectacled and naked, pushing a woman on a swing, also naked. I've always imagined him giving a thumbs-up but I can't confirm this because I've never actually seen the magazine.

But most shockingly of all, I knew that Johnny got into porn to find a girlfriend.

To me, this idea was always the most difficult to grasp. It seemed the most implausible. What kind of cockamamy plan was this from a man who got accepted to UNC from out of state? It's common enough for people to spend their whole lives building careers or amassing wealth in order to get laid. So one could argue that Johnny had cleverly skipped the middleman. His career *was* to get laid. Which is all well and good—unless that was never the point. Unless Johnny only ever wanted to cuddle and spoon and take turns spitting toothpaste into a bathroom sink. What if all those lawn orgies and park-bench encounters were constructed solely for Johnny to find love? For years, I thought about this every time I sat on a park bench. Until one day, when I couldn't stand thinking about it anymore.

* * *

"What do you need his e-mail address for?"

My parents are skeptical about me contacting Johnny. They have spent most of my life portraying this man as a caricature, but when push comes to shove, Johnny is suddenly quite three-dimensional. They don't want me pestering a seventy-four-year-old man with stunt-cock inquiries.

"He's a very sweet person," adds my mother.

"What is it you think I'm going to do to him?"

The truth is I don't know exactly what I want from Johnny. Certainly, an academic curiosity about pornography is not a revelation. What am I going to do, blow the lid off fake orgasms? Nor is a sociological curiosity. David Foster Wallace wrote at length about the Adult Video News Awards, thus pissing a circle around the subject for all eternity. My only credential is that I am a blood relative. But even this is a lame justification. People related to politicians, for instance, don't get more insight into them than the rest of us. If anything, they get less.

At least some portion of Johnny's draw comes from my own coastal turmoil. I have often felt I was mistakenly born a mid-Atlantic baby. I'm happy in San Francisco and have taught myself to be happy in Los Angeles. But after a few weeks, some tendril pokes up from my core and says: "You can't stay here, you'll go crazy." And so I come back east, feeling smug and sane, having taken advice from a talking tendril. Yet the more I heard of Johnny's "running off to California," the more I felt a kinship with this person over my family.

But I can't tell my parents any of that. So I play the mortality card instead.

"He won't be around forever," I say.

"Neither will we," my father says. "And we're interesting!"

"Not that interesting," my mother corrects him, and forks over the e-mail.

* * *

Johnny writes back right away. It's nice to hear from me, but he's hesitant to chat. He needs to mull it over. I tell him to take his time, mull away, no problem. In truth, I am surprised. Not because I expect him to expose himself emotionally as he has physically, but because he has been a public participant in his former life. Only a few years ago, he was inducted into the Legends of Erotica Hall of Fame in Las Vegas. No one in my family was told about it, but during a recent Google search I read how a former colleague introduced him as "the most important person in all of Northern California during porn's golden age; the guy who literally taught me how to fuck on camera—and this was before Viagra!" (The invocation of Viagra seems to be the porn industry equivalent of telling a younger person that you used to walk uphill to and from school, both ways.) At the end of the ceremony, the host wheeled out a block of cement for Johnny to stick his septuagenarian penis into. He demurred and signed his name instead.

A full month later, Johnny's name reappears in my in-box along with the subject line "apologies." Of course, "apologies." Of course, I should never have contacted him. I should have done as my parents suggested and let the man live his life. But Johnny is only apologizing for the delay. He was in Ojai and off e-mail. Ojai, I think. He has a place in the mountains! A place he can escape to or at least visit. He is not sad, he is happy. One rumor debunked already. Ojai. That's where they have the turtle sanctuary. I imagine Johnny stepping out of a sun-dappled ranch house. The air is perfumed with flowers as he heads out on his morning turtle feed. I imagine him sitting on one of the great big ones, being carried in slow motion across a green meadow. Then I imagine him doing all of this naked and giving a thumbs-up.

And so I stop imagining and get on a plane.

* * *

Reality is quick to replace fantasy. This is true in every arena except for sex, where pornography has more or less ruined sex for
all men under thirty. But it remains true that once you visit a
place, it's almost impossible to replicate the images you had of
that place before you went. As I stand across the street from
Johnny's apartment complex in Culver City, I make a mental note
of what I think it might look like inside. From my febrile imagination, I conjure a time capsule of the seventies—faux wood pan-
eling, disco records, memorabilia and awards. Maybe a sunken
living room. Maybe a sex swing. Maybe a wicker sex swing.

Johnny comes out into the hallway to greet me as I step off
the elevator. He is shorter than I am, soft-spoken, with a shy grin.
Some people are more comforting to look at than others and
Johnny is one of them. He has a face like the man in the moon.
He's also noticeably spry. I pick up the pace and follow him to his
apartment. He opens the door to an aseptic one-bedroom with
white carpeting that stops at the kitchen. The counters are over-
run with rows of vitamin bottles. In the living room sits a white
sofa, white sitting chairs and a white table with a glass bowl of
fruit on it. Angled on a small piano are framed photographs of his
nieces and nephews, a family that is not quite mine. This is the
apartment of a dental hygienist. There is, however, a curious
amount of exercise equipment.

"I like to stay fit," Johnny says.

The place is laden with bars and bells and core-strengthening
mousetraps. Two purple balls take over the whole sofa like giant

dogs. Across the bedroom door frame is a pull-up bar, gleaming in the sunlight. Johnny removes a hand gripper from one of the chairs and offers me a blueberry. I sit and sigh. Then he sits and sighs. We then proceed to talk about his brother's cockatoo for what feels like ten minutes. This is my doing. I'm the one who broached the subject of the cockatoo. When I was nineteen, I spent an afternoon with the Paris-dwelling doctor while backpacking across Europe. We sat on his balcony, drinking tea, while the cockatoo sprawled out on his lap, getting the underside of its wing scratched.

Johnny informs me of the cockatoo's recent demise. I thought they lived forever, like African gray parrots. Apparently they have an average aviary lifespan.

"Do you think he'll get another one?" I ask.

"Oh, I don't think so," says Johnny. "I think the cockatoo was burdensome, shrieking every time the phone rang."

Have I flown to Los Angeles to make a retired porn star say "cockatoo" over and over? People go to Los Angeles for less.

"I'm don't know why I'm here," I confess.

"That's okay," Johnny says, gracious and smiling.

I had said those words to myself many times en route—at airport security, while stomping through the empty tennis-ball can of a Jetway, in the bathroom at LAX, plugging Johnny's address into my phone—but saying them out loud, I realize just how untrue they are. Deep down, I know exactly why I have come and it is not because I have a California fetish. It's because, like Johnny, I have been looking for love in all the wrong places.

While I have not been frequenting strip clubs in the hopes of snagging a soul mate, I have become increasingly attracted to unrealistic or unobtainable men. I have broken things off with them or vice versa but each relationship feels quicker than the one before it. This is a problem everyone I know seems to have encountered in their twenties but has spontaneously outgrown in their thirties. One day you look around and the most romantically remedial people imaginable are signing leases with whole human beings, getting wistful about their former proclivities for drunks and sociopaths. I attempt to participate in these conversations, nodding along. How stupid we all once were! But I am only thinking of the phone in my pocket, where some cleverly flirtatious text might await me. I am in my mid-thirties and I seem to be working in reverse, going from long relationships that aren't wonderful to short relationships that aren't horrible.

So I have come to see Johnny the same way masochistic parents make their children smoke an entire pack of cigarettes if they catch them smoking one. I want to stare into the face of a single man, forty years my senior, who's been looking for love in the most unlikely place imaginable. I am in search of well-earned wisdom, of someone to smack me out of my habits. Like a vaccination, I am hoping that by immersing myself in an extreme version of my problem, I can be cured of my problem. But seeing as how our longest conversation ever has been about a dead bird, I hold off on sharing this revelation. Instead, we start at the beginning.

* * *

Johnny was born in 1943 in New Rochelle, New York, where he was a good student but not a great one. His younger brothers quickly surpassed him in athletic and academic prowess. Not that

Johnny would have known. His mother instructed his brothers to lie about their trophies and their grades—even to physically hunch on occasion—to protect Johnny's feelings. Which is an efficient way to mess up multiple children at once. Johnny learned that he was living in his own personal *Truman Show* during college, while home playing basketball with his youngest brother. For the first time, he didn't let Johnny win. Johnny was unable to compute the loss, so the brother explained everything. As one might imagine, Johnny was more than a little unmoored. Activities at which he'd always excelled were called into question. He wondered if he had any talent at all.

Then, in 1965, he was drafted. This upset him because he was seeing a therapist who he liked and he hadn't "completed the therapy." Therapy, understandably, was paramount to Johnny. Less understandable is the fact that most of the family saw the same therapist when he was growing up. He remembers riding a Schwinn to go see a psychiatrist. When I ask him if he was given a specific reason, he says therapy was like "brushing your teeth," just some Salingery exercise in which the whole family partook.

"So how long did you stay in therapy?"

"I stopped a couple of months ago. My therapist was older than I am, which is hard to find at my age."

"Oh," I say, "I'm sorry."

"He's not dead," Johnny corrects me. "He just thought I was cured."

"Of what?"

"Of my problems," he says, smiling coyly.

I theorize that since he started going to therapy before he had problems, perhaps it's therapy that gave him the problems. Like one of those lip balms secretly formulated to make your lips dry so you keep using it.

"That sounds paranoid," Johnny says.

Fair enough, I think. You reach six decades of therapy, you are officially allowed to diagnose anyone you choose.

After he got out of the military, Johnny packed up his car and moved to Fort Lauderdale to "figure out what life is all about." When I tell him that Fort Lauderdale is not a place generally associated with enlightenment, he tells me that's why he moved to Minneapolis. After Minneapolis came Denver, after Denver came San Francisco—and San Francisco is where his life cracked open.

"I arrived in 1970 and everyone was openly smoking pot and I thought, Wow, this is pretty wild. At first, I was living in a residents' club. It was cheap and you got to meet a whole new group of people before everyone went in different directions. It was really delightful."

Only a small percentage of the population speaks of shared toilets with such fondness. Then again, an even smaller percentage of nice Jewish boys from Westchester go into the adult film industry. But Johnny has a way of imbuing everything with positive thinking. On his castmates' orgasms: "I would wager a high percentage of them faked it but hey, what can you do?" On his niche notoriety: "I was just so happy knowing the women were happy with me." On John Holmes: "Private guy. Upbeat!" Johnny's first job in San Francisco was selling cable subscriptions door-to-door. And guess what? He friggin' loved it.

"The cable company was required by law to have a channel that was available to the public."

"A public-access channel?"

"Yes, one of those. And they needed a host. So I wound up interviewing people, and they supplied me with a cameraman. I interviewed exotic dancers and artists. They filmed me getting a massage. One day I interviewed this guy who published a magazine for the Sexual Freedom League and I was intrigued. They had some wild parties—nude parties, sex parties—and I attended those."

"Attended," I interject, adding air quotes.

Johnny looks at me as if I'm trying to sexualize a trip to the mailbox.

"Anyway, I started distributing the league's magazine in vending machines. I had never even seen an adult film at that point. So I went to a theater downtown and I was awed by what these people were doing up on the screen."

Awed is what most people feel when they see the northern lights or Meryl Streep. And yet I wholly believe Johnny when he says it, just like I believe him when he says he then said to himself, "My God, that woman seems to be having a great time! How do I get in on that?"

Turns out, the answer was at hand. The paper Johnny distributed was covering the trial of the Mitchell brothers, who, already famous for producing live sex shows, were in hot water for making a film during which a priest sticks his penis through a confession box and gets a blow job. Because the world was a different place in 1972, the paper saw fit to print the physical address of the Mitchell brothers' offices. Years later, one brother would shoot the other in the face, an incident that, among other tragic consequences, fated them to be played by Charlie Sheen and Emilio Estevez in a made-for-TV movie—but first, they had to contend with a determined young man by the name of Johnny Seeman.

Johnny knocked on their office door one day and explained that he wanted to have sex on camera. He left out the part where he also wanted to take his costar to a candlelit dinner and ask her about her hopes and dreams.

"They took one look at me and laughed in my face. I wasn't hip. I wasn't a flower child. I didn't have long hair. I was probably wearing what I'm wearing now."

He gestures down at high-waisted khaki pants, a belt and a short-sleeved button-down shirt. It's true. This is an unfuckable outfit if ever there was one. But Johnny persisted, coming back week after week until the Mitchell brothers relented. Mystifyingly, Johnny did not have to try out in any capacity. In *Boogie Nights*, Rollergirl fellates Dirk Diggler in the back of a club before recommending him to the director. While I do not assume real porn casting is all blowjobs and roller skates, dropping one's pants seems like it would be industry standard. But apparently all you had to do in this pre-AIDS, post-sexual-revolution flesh carnival was hop into the back of a VW bus and drive to a house in Walnut Creek.

When Johnny arrived, two men and a woman were already waiting, lounging naked on a circular sofa. Upon seeing this scene, he and his priapic penis became anxious about the straw they were about to draw.

"I told them I was heterosexual and they told me not to worry. They said, 'You're all just going to be relating to her at the same time.'"

"Relating," I interject again, once more with the air quotes. No response.

"I was so nervous," Johnny says, "I had to pee every fifteen minutes while they were setting up. Then I couldn't get an erection on camera. They had to shoot the whole thing around me."

In the end, they gave him seventy-five dollars and, to Johnny's surprise, a second chance. This time with just him and one woman. And that was all he needed. So strong was Johnny's desire for a steady relationship, even his dick was in on the plan. And while a relationship never did manifest, a career did. Before long, Johnny was a regular in movies. Then he began managing productions. Then he became a line producer (this was when there were lines, before the dialogue had moved from "Nice shoes, wanna fuck?" to "Shoes"). Then he became a producer, coordinating with location scouts and catering people. (Prior to this moment, I had not imagined there would be catering on the set of adult films. Though it makes sense—sex requires more energy than a monologue unless you're doing both wrong.) When Johnny started directing his own films, his parents flew out to San Francisco for his first premiere.

"What did your mother think of it?"

I had always imagined my great-aunt's expression upon opening the dirty magazine, and it didn't jibe with her flying out to California to support her son. She was one of those mannered ladies with flawless taste in clothing, husbands, and houses. After she died, her wine collection went to auction. And while the idea of some scandalized East Coast lady in a San Francisco porn theater is appealing in the abstract, I couldn't picture this particular East Coast lady there.

"She had a one-word review," Johnny says. "She found it 'repetitious.'"

This is as fair an assessment of pornography as I've ever heard. "But she was proud?"

"She was relieved. She liked me being on the other side of the camera."

* * *

All Uncle Johnny wanted was to take his work home with him. Which, in a way, he did. Just not in the way he'd hoped. He got to know the industry so well, he made "a booklet of tips" for guys getting into porn for the first time. When I ask him if it was called "Just the Tips," he stares at me blankly. It dawns on me that Johnny's life has been so chock a block with sex jokes, he doesn't have the capacity to let another one in. His innuendo days are over. Instead, he tells me about how he took these guys under his wing and taught them how to fuck on camera. He speaks with such fondness for his costars that I am momentarily transported, forgetting that knowing how to fuck on camera is not a life skill.

"We ate dinner on each other's porches," he says. "Everyone thought we were having orgies but never. We just . . . we just really liked each other."

I tell him what I know to be true: He was adored by these people. I've read the interviews. I've been reading them for years.

"Yeah," he whispers, "that was my world. We were outlaws together."

He means that literally. San Francisco was the hot spot for

porn. In Los Angeles, police would drive around, following the actors, raiding sets. Tailing porn stars was a trickier business in a semi-walkable city. They could film where and when they wanted. For the most part. Once Johnny was part of a crew that borrowed a Rolls-Royce and drove up to Mill Valley to shoot a sex scene on a hill overlooking the city. Johnny was in the film, in the midst of "doing crazy sexual things" to Annette Haven, one of the industry's more famous faces.

"We were on the trunk, on the roof, on the motor, inside the car, on the—"

"I got it."

"The next thing you know, a police officer comes charging out of the woods and yells, 'Nobody move!' We were taken down to the station for public indecency, but when we got there, Annette just spent hours signing autographs for the cops."

Johnny laughs. I laugh. Finally, I see my opening.

"So did you ever date Annette? After that?"

"She had a boyfriend," he says. "And it wasn't like that."

"Right," I say. "But did you ever want to date one of your costars?"

"You mean like was I in love with one of them?"

I put my fist to my mouth and clear my throat. "I was under the impression that you got into porn to find a girlfriend."

"Ah," he says. "It's true. I was always scheming about how to make one of these women my girlfriend. I know it's not the standard reason people do this. A lot of people I knew were aspiring actors or models. Mainstream Hollywood was getting more risqué and porn was getting longer scripts and so they thought eventually it would meet in the middle. They thought they were going to be needed. But they weren't needed. And then it was just—over. But I was looking for a relationship."

"Did you ever find one?"

"I haven't dated a woman for more than three months my entire life," he says, popping a blueberry into his mouth. "The last time I had sex was the night Mike Tyson bit Evander Holyfield's ear off."

"And you haven't dated anyone for longer than three months since then?"

"Nope."

The irony of this is not lost on Johnny. He runs a singles group at his local temple. He spends half his days helping other people find love.

"I hate to say this, but I think it's the ultimate form of going after something you can't have. If people become available to me in a real way, I think: How could they be interested? How could I have been interested in them? When I was working, I'd feel a connection with someone but then she'd start having sex with someone else who was taller and better-looking and I thought: I can't compare to that guy."

This is a familiar scenario for anyone living in the world, but Johnny subjected himself to the experience in real time. When he says "start having sex with someone else," he means on the same piece of furniture.

Johnny made his last film in 1987. He was really attracted to the woman he was paired with and thought she might, at long last, make a good girlfriend. Then it turned out she already had a boyfriend and said boyfriend was a Hells Angel.

"I thought, well, that's not going anyplace."

"And that was the last straw? After a decade of this?"

"It would have been nice for it to come earlier," Johnny agrees, "but I guess I'm a slow learner."

He looks at me for the first time without blinking or smiling, just dead-on like he knows exactly why I'm here.

"You don't just stop being who you are when you reach a certain age. You know that, right? You don't magically outgrow yourself. The life you're living now is your actual life, the habits you have now are your actual habits. I hope I've evolved—but I'm not so sure. But I can tell you that if you're setting things up so they never work out by picking the wrong partners and you know you're doing it . . ."

Johnny trails off. He looks at the photos on the piano.

"Yes?" I ask.

"Just stop it," he says.

* * *

Johnny has never watched himself on-screen. He doesn't own a single copy of his films and the idea of going to some retro-themed website holds no appeal. He thinks the Internet is plenty masturbatory without having to watch himself have sex on it. He is happy enough knowing that his movies are out there, that there's proof he was the best ever at something, which is more than most people get. He recently told his piano teacher. They were swapping stories about their younger selves and Johnny was growing uncomfortable with all those unaccounted-for years. So, wary as he was, he told her. But when he saw her again the following week, the first thing she did was advise him not to go around telling people about his "film career."

Having finally gotten to know the real Johnny, I am livid on his behalf. Who was this woman to go around passing out scarlet letters? Stick with "Chopsticks," sweetheart, and leave the moral shaming to the religious right. But Johnny took it in stride. He knew the risks of sharing in advance. In fact, he knows how lucky he is—Johnny's particular brand of fame means he can deploy his history at will, pluck it out of obscurity or keep it buried.

"It will always be mine," he explains. "It may be a red flag but it's my red flag. Like I said, this is my actual life. This is the one I chose."

It's getting dark out. Johnny walks me into the hall, where a halogen light flickers above our heads. He presses the elevator button for me. Nothing is revolutionary about Johnny's advice. It feels as if I've always known it. Which is the flawed nature of all advice—you can have all the wisdom in the world laid out for you but it takes a lifetime to apply it. But just because Johnny's plan didn't work doesn't mean it was ill-advised. His costars weren't undatable by virtue of their profession. He just kept relating to them in a way that made them impossible to date.

"Hey," Johnny says, moving in front of the elevator doors as they open, "you want to hear a dirty joke?"

"Sure," I say, stunned that he knows any.

"How many porn stars does it take to change a lightbulb?"

"How many?"

"One," he says, and grins. "So long as he screws it in himself."

Brace
Yourself

I GO TO FRANCE. I GO BECAUSE I AM RESEARCHING A NOVEL THAT takes place in a château in the middle of nowhere in Normandy. I chose my topic wisely but not conveniently. It's tough to locate "the middle of nowhere" in a country the size of France, but I managed to do it.

My friend Charlotte, a photographer interested in unmarked WWII graves, accompanies me. Charlotte is the kind of magnetically stunning, deeply chill person who lives on Earth, true, but on a parallel Earth. Hers is a planet where people stock your phone with adoring text messages at all hours and pump your gas for you even when you're not in New Jersey. This would be infuriating if it weren't for the fact that Charlotte so thoroughly inhabits her version of Earth that her mind will not allow for a lesser version. Of course you live here, too, she thinks, slipping on special jeans meant for people with stilts for legs. Why *wouldn't* you easily finagle a free trip to Japan? Why *wouldn't* the coffee shop accept your credit card even though there's a 10 DOLLAR MINIMUM CHARGE sign? Why *wouldn't* every member of the opposite sex realize that they had never known beauty before they laid eyes on you?

The family who owns the château agrees to let us stay in their guest quarters at a discount. I tell Charlotte the good news.

"Did you mention the novel?" she asks.

This is Charlotte math. Free is the favor. The discount is what comes with existing.

Twenty-four hours into our stay, Charlotte decides the place has bad juju. She's not wrong. The château's been around since the 1300s—someone definitely got the rack here—but her spiritual awareness has a way of appearing at convenient times. Such as when she would like to take the car for a week to go to Deauville, an artists' resort by the sea, to have impossibly hot sex with an impossibly good-looking sculptor. In the world I inhabit, the words *artist*, *resort*, and *good-looking* have never met before. In Charlotte's, they're old friends. I make her feel bad about this for a full minute before confessing that being alone is actually more conducive to writing. But it's too late—the seeds of guilt have been sown. She is abandoning me. She feels compelled to stock up on provisions so I don't have to *Les Miz* scraps of bread from the kitchen.

We go supermarket shopping and split up. I return to the parking lot to discover my friend is a Jewish mother trapped in a model's body. She has purchased a gallon of peanut butter, a wheel of cheese, crackers, frozen shrimp, chocolate bars, several bunches of root vegetables, dried apricots, three baguettes the size of pool noodles, and a 24-pack of bottled water. I tell her that the war is over. She, of all people, should know this.

"But what if you get hungry?" she asks.

She worries about this condition I have that requires me to eat food. I encourage her to take a baguette for the road.

"It's okay," she says. "They only charged me for one."

Back at the château, the impossibly good-looking sculptor calls. Charlotte takes the call, languidly leaning on a stone wall as I unload the trunk. A young tour guide emerges from the gatehouse and offers to help me with the groceries. My head in the trunk, I accept, but when I look up, I see she is sporting a neck brace from chin to chest. There was no neck brace this time yesterday.

"*Qu'est-ce qui s'est passé?*" I ask her.

Between my bad French and her bad English, I gather that last night she was backing her car out of a barn, moved to avoid a horse—or possibly a pile of hair—and rammed straight into a tree.

"It's okay," she concludes, reaching for a bag. "It doesn't hurt."

"No, please." I shoo her away.

"It's okay, really," she insists.

I shoo, she lunges, and we go back and forth like this—shoo, lunge, shoo, lunge—for whole minutes. Imagine trying to hold open a door for someone who refuses to take you up on the offer but now replay that exchange for the duration of a presidential debate. I don't know if it's the language barrier or stubbornness or what, but the conversation morphs from charming joust to forceful assertion to performance art. Meanwhile, Charlotte is pacing around a topiary, giggling and saying something enthusiastic about green tea.

I let the guide win. If carrying a 24-pack of water makes her feel empowered against trees, so be it. With a big grunt, she lifts several bags from the trunk. Just then, the owner of the château comes charging out of some French doors. Or, as they say in France, doors.

"*Non, non.*" She waves. "She is injured! Can't you see?"

We freeze. There's really no arguing with this. Of course she is injured. I am American, not Martian—I know what a neck brace looks like. Muscles pumping with anger, the woman yanks the bags out of the girl's hands and speed-walks toward the house without so much as looking me in the eye. I want the girl to explain how I refused her help and the conversational tug-of-war that followed. But the phone starts ringing in the gatehouse and so she turns around to attend to it as if nothing happened. I am left standing in the driveway at the center of a triangle of women, all walking away from me at different paces. I lift the remaining bag from the trunk and shuffle toward the main house, where I will live for the next seven days, the Ugly American sitting in her room, her wheel of cheese taking up an entire shelf in the refrigerator.

Immediate
Family

YOU GET TO KNOW ALL THE OLD PEOPLE. THIS IS WHAT NO ONE tells you when you decide to work from home, but it's true. One generation's "off-peak hours" is another's "hours." There they are, walking their rickety dogs at ten, doing their laundry at noon, checking their mail at three, asking you if you know how to operate a VCR machine at six.

You can be ill at ease with this, seeing it as a premature separation from your rightful generation, or you can embrace it. Marilyn helped me embrace it. She complained about the slow elevator and taught me how to trick the dryer into running an extra load, free. She was always late for the opera. She was feisty—

a word my peers employ when describing people who curse after the age of eighty. And then one day, according to an index card taped to the lobby wall, she was dead.

Blue ink announced that the family would be sitting shiva in her apartment. It listed the hours, the days, and finally, in block letters: ALL FRIENDS AND NEIGHBORS WELCOME. I did a double take. Was Marilyn not selling me on the wonders of dryer sheets a mere two days ago?

My first thought: I should go. For one thing, I am Jewish and have been to plenty of shivas before, so that would take some of the awkwardness out of it. My second thought: I should definitely not go. I had lived in the building for only seven months. I barely knew this person.

Part of what's interesting about living in New York is how much business you can choose to have with people who are absolutely none of your business. There's something incongruous about how careful we are to set up boundaries, how ardent we are about maintaining them, and how quick we are to take a wrecking ball to them when it suits us. We train one another to disengage at the daily level, to greet with silent nods, to ignore music coming through the walls or tearful phone calls on the street. Yet when we want to feel we're doing the right thing, we come swooping in with eye contact and directions.

It's not that I had ignored Marilyn. I liked Marilyn. But I wasn't about to invite her to dinner or ask her if she had grandkids or engage her a moment longer than I had to. I work from home, after all. I need my space. Now tragedy had struck and I was going to, what—buy a fruit plate and go sit down with a stranger's family?

In the end, I made my decision the way I make all decisions I've brutalized with analysis—by giving up and awaiting logistical intervention. On the second night of the shiva, a friend requested that we move our drinks date to a dinner date, thus giving me a clear window of time to brush my hair and walk upstairs.

When I opened the door, I was so distracted by the fact that Marilyn's apartment could eat my apartment for breakfast, I nearly forgot why I had come. I made my way down a long hallway, through the mourners eating pastrami, and found a woman directly related to Marilyn.

"Was it sudden?" I asked after introducing myself.

"Oh no," said the woman. "It was pneumonia. It had been going on for months."

"I'm so sorry," I said, shaking my head. "I just can't believe it."

Had I not seen her, just last week, lecturing a new tenant about cigarette butts?

"Aren't you sweet to come?" the woman said, grabbing my arm and insisting I squeeze in on the sofa. "But he lived a long life."

"Who he?"

"Our father."

"Who art in heaven?"

"My father."

"Marilyn's husband?"

The woman cocked her head and blinked at me. Now the whole family was listening.

"I'm Marilyn," she said, putting her hand to her chest. "My father died. We're sitting shiva for him."

Lenore. Lenore is the name of the feisty lady who helped me

with the dryer. Ageism is a horrible thing that can appear in many guises. But unlike the more sinister sister isms, one of the symptoms is not thinking that all old people look alike. And yet, here we were.

This is the danger of deciding, too late, to be a good neighbor, to care because you think you should. Extricating myself from the situation required a social deftness that I did not possess. I stayed for eleven minutes. As I left, Marilyn offered me food, which I was too embarrassed to accept. I had dinner plans and also a hunch that she thought I had secretly come for the food. We chatted about the building and the upcoming election and she couldn't have been nicer, suggesting that maybe we were meant to be friends as well as neighbors.

"Well, I'll never forget your name," I said, apologizing again, hugging her and slinking back down the stairs.

At the mailboxes the next afternoon, I ran into Lenore. Because I was checking my mail in the middle of the day. Because I have become one of them. But I still have my boundaries. So when Lenore exclaimed, "Look at all this junk mail, it's enough to kill me!" I only nodded. I did not tell her that I thought it had, in fact, killed her. When it comes to death, it's better to live and let live.

Cinema
of
the
Confined

THE BED IS SPINNING IN CIRCLES AND I CAN'T MAKE IT STOP. I wake in the middle of the night to this sensation. It's as if a basketball-playing giant has broken into my room, balanced the mattress on his fingertip and started pushing for his own depraved amusement. Petrified, I sit up straight as they do in horror films and gasp. The movement crests and fades, but it lasts long enough for me to pinpoint the direction in which I am whirling (clockwise). I try convincing myself there is nothing wrong with me. Earlier that evening, I had been speaking to students at Trinity College. Perhaps I can blame the disorientation on sleeping in a New England guesthouse. This is not my doily-covered bed.

Those are not my porcelain bird figurines. But when I lie back down, the spinning begins again. There's no denying it: This is full-tilt vertigo.

When you have vertigo—or, more accurately, are subject to its whims—there is no protracted period of time during which you confuse it for something else, like being drunk or getting up too quickly. Not to withhold empathy from those who make a habit of lying down and getting back up again, but if you think you might have experienced vertigo, you likely have not. Unlike your garden-variety dizziness, vertigo is debilitating and surprising. Your brain processes it the same way it might process, say, being punched awake. It had also happened to me before (the vertigo, not the punching). The first time was after a breakup, during which it became the physical manifestation of a life spinning out of control—alas, there is no known cure for symbolism—and the second was while hiking along a ravine in Big Sur, California. I realize that sounds like something I made up, like having a heart attack in the card aisle of a pharmacy on Valentine's Day. But you know what else sounds made up? Vertigo.

Before I dabbled in it myself, I didn't think it was a medical condition any more than I thought the willies were a medical condition. My sole association was the Hitchcock film. If you've seen *Vertigo*, you'll know this is a movie that not only has little to do with the condition, but stretches the limits of believability in general: A stunning twenty-five-year-old woman throws herself at an unemployed fifty-year-old man and San Francisco is entirely devoid of traffic. These are but two of the many reasons they don't show *Vertigo* in medical school. The *trailer* for the film, on the other hand, rings as true as tinnitus. A prop dictionary is flipped open and the camera zooms in on the entry for *vertigo*: "A state in which all things seem to be engulfed in a whirlpool of terror."

* * *

On the train back to New York, I watched telephone wires bob and smokestacks billow as I focused on Long Island Sound. Once my body discovers it can do something—get a weird rash, have a sinus infection, eat an entire block of cheese in one sitting—it's liable to do that thing again. What I did not want was to become dizzy on a fast-moving object. I imagined it would be like when a moving subway car passes your still one and you experience the somewhat embarrassing sensation of momentum. *Are we mov—? Oh. Never mind.*

As soon as I got home, I made an appointment with an ear, nose, and throat doctor whose last name is Goldfinger. I had seen Dr. Goldfinger in the past and knew him to be one of those rare doctors who maintained a balance* between treating you like a person and treating you like *The New England Journal of Medicine*. I also knew him to have a humongous painting of a Rorschach test in his waiting room. Please allow me to correct the image in your mind: The words RORSCHACH TEST are spelled out in giant letters.

Because it had been many years since my last visit, I was given a clipboard with a frosting-thick pile of forms to fill out. Bending my head invited the spins, so I slouched in my chair until my chin was parallel with my knees and leaned the clipboard against

---

*I would apologize, but it's definitely going to happen again.

them. A woman seated across from me glared in my direction, but an old man in a tweed cap had a smile for me. Boy, had he been there before! I knew I should have been grateful for this twinkle of commiseration, for this moment of kindness passed from one generation to the next. But I don't want to be part of any club that can't remember its own handshake.

I clicked a cheap pink pen meant to resemble an esophagus and began filling in the blanks, of which there were many. Doctor's office forms are a poor example of what we, as a society, are capable of. For starters, why are they on paper? Even the most avowed Luddite will concede that information like "Sulfur makes my throat close up" should not be subject to a mortal medium like handwriting. Also, why do they need your social security number fifty times? Are these forms being scattered to the four corners of the earth? Is one getting buried in a time capsule? Can I see the capsule? And "Who should we contact in case of emergency?" Well. I'm already *at* a doctor's office.

* * *

Dr. Goldfinger hadn't aged a day in the decade since last I'd seen him. This was not necessarily a good thing. True, he didn't look a day over forty-eight, but he had also never looked a day under forty-eight. I'd seen photos. Either way, I was relieved to be in his presence. I knew he could help me because last time, he'd performed the Epley, a maneuver familiar to all vertigo sufferers. The Epley is often misspelled as "Epily," the first half of the Latin word *epilepsia*. It should go without saying that vertigo is to epi-

lepsy as the willies are to vertigo. But our brains are catastro-
phists, even when it comes to spelling.

The Epley is the only known way to alleviate BPPV (benign
paroxysmal positional vertigo). Before the "benign" part erodes
your sympathy, I might remind you that, technically, losing a pin-
kie is benign. The Epley was invented in 1980, a detail I find
dubious in the same way I find the fresh ink in the Mormon
Bible dubious. What did dizzy people do before 1980? Floun-
der around until they slammed into a flagpole? Also, maneuvers
don't feel very medical. For all its complexity, the human body is
a finite terrain. There are only so many things one can do with
one's arms, for example. So if you've practiced yoga with any reg-
ularity, you have inadvertently Epleyed yourself.

What happens is this: You sit up straight and turn your head
toward whichever ear is causing you trouble. A doctor then
knocks you backward in the chair until you're horizontal. If you
have vertigo, you will experience the sensation of someone putting your brain in a washing machine and drying it out on a record player. Once this happens, the doctor turns your head in the
opposite direction. Done quickly, this is called murder. Done
slowly, it's called medicine. It's meant to dislodge sodium crystals
from where they have mischievously migrated—to your semicir-
cular ear canals—and back to the inner ear, where they belong.
Yes, crystals. In our ears. I know. We are all unicorns.

The only catch is that you then have to face perfectly forward
for the next twenty-four hours to allow the crystals to settle back
into place. You'd think these instructions would be easier to follow
in New York City, as most of us are not circling parking garages

or merging onto highways. Alas, taking the subway is pretty much out of the question. As is descending steps, jaywalking, ducking, or reacting to noise. Oh, and drop something on the floor? That's where that lives now. But twenty-four hours is a small price to pay for something that works.

Except that this time, it didn't.

After sleeping as instructed ("like a mummy": Dr. Goldfinger crossed his hands over his chest to be sure I got the picture), I woke up full of hope. I wanted to start the process of being thankful for my health so that I could go back to taking it for granted like a normal person. When we're sick or in pain, even if it's just a case of "something in the eye," we swear up and down that we will be grateful for every moment from this day forward when there is not something in our eye. I don't know with whom we're bargaining or with what lousy chips. But I could worry about that once the ceiling stopped melting into the walls.

Alas, the dizziness had not only worsened, it had mutated. Up until now, the vertigo attacks—or "spells," as I liked to call them when I wanted to make them adorable and Victorian—had been peppered with hours of normalcy during which I could work or pick up socks. Those hours were gone now. I tried to stand but fell backward. My vision blurred. It was like riding the teacups at Disney World, if Disney World was built on a fault line that shifted every fifteen minutes. I watched myself go through this with as much of a sense of curiosity as fear. The moment something goes wrong with you that has not gone wrong before, it seems at once tragic and temporary. Imagine if you had made it this far without getting a common cold and then you got one. You'd probably think you were dying. This is because the frightened brain becomes a binary place: It's "probably nothing" or you've contracted an incurable flesh-eating disease. That's it. Those are your options.

* * *

Writing about illness is a form of travel writing. The writer's mind stands at attention, even when her body cannot, because she has entered a new environment—in one case voluntarily, in the other not. Everything feels as if it's of note. As it is in travel writing, the difficulty is not in taking a small incident and expounding upon it but in whittling a new world down to a manageable size. Every article on kite surfing in Tahiti has a larger narrative behind it of flight delays, food poisoning, and fraught texts with an ex. The big difference between travel writing and medical writing is that those extra details do not lend themselves to repurposing. Not at a party, talking to your friend who's "super into weird medical shit," not with your mom, who's preprogrammed to care, not even with someone who turns out to have the same problem but would rather stick porcupine quills up her nail beds before revisiting it.

If you're the kind of person who gets off on daring people to be offended by a play-by-play of your mole removal, well, at least you're not boring people. But being sick for an extended period of time isn't about disgust—it's about tedium, which is like toxic mold to entertainment. And yet here is where the truth of the infirm lives, in those in-between spaces of bed/transit/medicine, medicine/transit/bed. Here is a parallel universe of hold music and water glasses and make-a-fist montages. *Come one, come all! Behold screenshots of my call logs to the insurance company!*

"This is what I'm dealing with," I typed, anger-forwarding the pictures to friends.

"That sucks!" they wrote back, because it did suck.

What else was there to say? It's not that people don't care, it's that they're not there. What's alluring about travel writing becomes repellent in medical writing. No one is asking to be "made jealous" by photos of your stitches. No one hears a rumor you've gone to Duane Reade and says, "Bring me back something." In response, those of us living on the wrong side of the hospital curtain pick over our own misery for trinkets that might amuse a healthy person. It's a form of digestion but it's also a form of regurgitation.

Here is my own best example of this: A while ago, my father was diagnosed with one of those ambitious cancers that demands a bone marrow transplant and quarantine. His doctors took away all his white blood cells and pumped him full of chemicals. (The trick with cancer is that you have to play dead in order to keep it from actually killing you.) He's in remission now, but this was the largest-scale medical disaster ever to hit our family. It was all we thought about for a year. Yet this is the only story I tell from that time: I was sitting with my father during one of his chemotherapy sessions, reading a trashy magazine as he was fiddling with his iPad, when a volunteer opened the door. She was holding a fistful of wildflowers, which I was pretty sure were contraband in a cancer ward.

"Good morning!" she said, in a high-pitched voice. "Would you like a flower?"

I looked at my father. Should I call security on this squeaky toy in a skirt? He thanked her, gestured around the room, and explained that he didn't have anywhere to put a flower. So she skipped off down the hallway. He returned to his e-mail, I to my magazine.

Then, without taking his eyes off the screen, he said:

"Wow, nothing says 'You're dying' like 'Here, have this fucking daisy.'"

* * *

Around and around and around I went. Dr. Goldfinger advised me to give it some time before coming back to his office. This was fine by me. My body was like a dreidel bomb that could go off any minute. Plus, his office is located on the Upper East Side, which is just a hive of doctors' offices. Cab rides to the Upper East Side should really count toward one's health insurance deductible. Alas, I moved too slowly and for no perceptible reason to take the subway. There wasn't much to be done besides wait it out. Vertigo is neither rare nor fatal. Something like 30 percent of Americans experience it. It can be a symptom of stress or teeth clenching. People on sedatives report waking up with it. Surfers get it if they fall on a wave at the wrong angle. Some women get it with their periods. Because periods are refugee camps for all nondescript maladies.

But then another week passed. And another. And another. Then four.

Plans fell like bowling pins until I stopped lining them up. I turned to the holistic, experimenting with breathing and oils. There's a Buddhist meditation in which the objective is to imagine the world on the head of a pin—but each time I tried, the world wound up on the tip of a conductor's baton. For the friends and loved ones who called or texted, I apologized for being MIA.

But I was neither missing nor in action. Just in. Some came over, carrying soup—a well-meaning gesture that reminded me of how ill-suited I was to my condition. My age bracket is trained to equate illness with the flu. People asked what more they could do and were disappointed when the answer was "Please mail these letters." Soup is the gesture of a hero. Letters are the errand of an intern. And for those who happened not to get in touch? I began to hold little grudges. At least now we knew who my real friends were, didn't we?

This is what comes of too much intimacy with one's ceiling.

Of all the indignities, showering was the worst. I was too young, with too many of my original teeth, to die a shower death. Other deaths, okay. Exploding manhole covers are ageless. But falling in the shower? Why don't I just charge up a mobility scooter and mow myself over with it now? But hygiene won out over dread. I got undressed, leaned on the tile with both hands, and let the water spill down the back of my neck.

Because I have seen too many movies during which people cry in the shower, I cried in the shower. Was this my life now? Would I only ever be able to walk two blocks and read half a magazine article? Pinning down the words was like removing shards of eggshell from a freshly cracked egg—possible but annoying. But mostly I cried because I was primed for hysteria. Unable to sleep without being spun awake, I had been indulging in the cinema of the confined. *The Diving Bell and the Butterfly, Murder in the First, Awakenings, The Sea Inside, Room,* and that most sacred of the claustrophobia canon, *The Boy in the Plastic Bubble.* I was a meticulous curator: trapped, bedridden, or abducted only. Stranded could suck it. Stranded was always temporary. Go crack open a fresh coconut and cry to NASA, you big babies.

I watched these movies because they presented a unifying tone, a myopic view of life in which there was no reality beyond their characters' predicaments. With most movies, be they grim dramas or romantic comedies, there is an invisible door to a different version of the world and the unspoken idea that everyone on-screen could just walk through it. Even when we are not explicitly told so, we know the characters in the dramas have seen the comedies and vice versa. The people in *Mystic River* have definitely seen *How to Lose a Guy in 10 Days*. They just have other things on their minds right now.

Not so in the claustrophobia canon. Those people haven't seen shit. They haven't laughed or texted or touched a blade of grass in years. When we watch these films, we adopt their experience, trying it on like a tight coat. And suddenly it's as if all the documentaries and romantic comedies and thrillers no longer exist, not for us and not for them. This is the essence of their appeal. We do not so much binge-watch them as purge-watch them, spewing the tapestry of our complicated lives onto their threadbare ones. It's why, if you are healthy, you walk out of the theater with a newfound appreciation for your life. And if you are unhealthy? It's as if someone has put horse blinders on you for a couple hours and said, "Here, miss the world a little less."

* * *

Then it was six weeks. Everything slowed to a crawl. I'd written nothing. Well, almost nothing. A nameless document on my computer read:

The desire to be healthy is different from the desire not to be sick.

Sheryl @ BlueCross

One assumes those lines are operating on two distinct planes of thought. I don't think Sheryl @ BlueCross told me that. Though, really, she could have.

* * *

I made my way back to Dr. Goldfinger, who had me walk up and down his hallway, touching my nose. The only conclusion he drew was that I was definitely sober. I did not tell him that I had also managed to cheat on him with a second ENT, who had unceremoniously shoved a fiber-optic cable up my nostrils and gave me no new information in return. It felt tawdry, leaving my co-pay on someone else's nightstand. This woman billed herself as an "ear specialist." It saddened me to think of Dr. Goldfinger knowing precisely one-third as much about the human ear.

"I think we should send you for an MRI," Dr. Goldfinger said, as I walked back to him in a straight line. "Just to rule things out."

"Yes," I agreed, "let us rule out all the things."

* * *

The severity of any medical condition can be measured in paper clothing. If you're given an open-backed gown, you're fine. If you're given an open-backed gown and a giant napkin, you're fine but you're at the gynecologist's office. So that's not ideal. If you're given an open-backed gown and paper slippers, you're in a hospital. If you're given an open-backed gown, paper slippers, and a hair cap, your organs are about to be harvested because you're a clone of a wealthier person who needs your parts.

"What's this for?" I asked, clutching the hair cap.

"Safety," the technician replied, a catchall for every object ever invented.

Getting one's hair caught inside the tracks of an MRI machine is just the kind of nightmare scenario that should have made it into the movies by now. Just look what modern cinema has done with the tanning bed—and there's nothing wrong with those characters aside from their desire to get into a tanning bed.

I knew the trick was to keep my eyes closed so that I didn't see the proximity of a coffin lid to my face. Just before he slid me in, the technician handed me a button with a cord attached "in case." In case I had a panic attack and needed to be yanked out. I was also given foam earplugs to dampen the noise. Foam earplugs are the gummy vitamins of soundproofing—you'd have to pour cement in your ears not to hear an MRI. I pretended I was at some kind of art installation, maybe at the Guggenheim, where one floor melds into the next. The first floor sounded like a game-show buzzer. The second, like ducks quacking while someone scrubbed tiles with steel wool. The top floor was a train barreling over the tracks of a small town. Then, suddenly, the noises stopped and the technician's voice came through a speaker:

"We happy in there?"

"Yes?" I guessed.

Realizing my synapses were on display on the other side of the wall, I began trying to stimulate them. I imagine this is about as effective as running around the block before a physical. I counted backward from 200. I engaged in disturbing thought experiments like: Who would I save in a fire, my cat or the uppity barista at my coffee shop? I tried replicating the feelings of infatuation I felt for ex-boyfriends, taking imaginary tours of their apartments, trying to remember which posters and paintings had gone on which walls. All in the name of having attractive synapses. Which, come to think of it, is just the kind of thinking that ended most of those relationships.

Afterward, I waited for Dr. Goldfinger in his office, studying the medical degrees hanging proudly above the hazardous-waste bin. During my last visit, I had made a point of complimenting his pants. They were brown with blue pinstripes. Very stylish for a doctor. Then it dawned on both of us that the reason I had the chance to study them was because he had just rotated my head parallel with his crotch.

"Thank you," Dr. Goldfinger said, clearing his throat. "They're Banana Republic."

"Well, they're great," I said, addressing his penis. "Do you have them in different colors?"

I could not, for the life of me, stop talking about the pants. I vowed to keep my mouth shut this time. So when he came in sporting a pair of red corduroys, I tried not to smile.

"I have some not-so-hot news," he announced.

Then I didn't have to try. Dr. Goldfinger explained that, after ruling out everything else and factoring in my range of symptoms, it was clear I had more than vertigo. The good news: I did not have a brain tumor. The bad news: I do have a funny little disease called Ménière's, which sounds like a pastry but is the opposite of a pastry.

Dr. Goldfinger explained that, unlike vertigo, Ménière's disease is relatively rare. There are about 200,000 cases in the United States. Though I will say 200,000 feels like an awful lot when you're one of them. In addition to the vertigo, the hallmarks of Ménière's are a feeling of fullness in the ears (as if they need to be popped), relentless dizziness, and spontaneous vomiting. There is no cure and no one can predict the duration of an attack. Some people get it for hours, others for years. Attacks amass over time, damaging the cilia in your inner ear a little more, culminating in deafness.

"Sorry, what?"

Dr. Goldfinger twisted on his rolling stool.

"Van Gogh had Ménière's," he offered.

And look how that turned out, I thought.

Naturally, I was upset. The idea of having something so permanent is upsetting. But in the moment, it felt more like a surprise adoption. As if this disease had been living its life somewhere else, with someone else, and due to unforeseen circumstances, I was now its guardian. I could not understand that it was a part of me, but I could understand that it would entail a change of plans. Which might explain why my first reaction was to tell Dr. Goldfinger that I had recently decided to become proficient in a musical instrument, specifically the violin. I felt my life would be greatly enriched if I could learn to play just one piece. Now what was I supposed to do?

"You're concerned with how this might affect your prospects for playing an instrument you've never played?"

"I played it in the third grade," I corrected him.

"Well, I wouldn't spend too much time thinking about that. People with severe Ménière's are on disability. They're really screwed. You have a low-grade version of the disease."

"Ménière's lite?" I asked, hopeful, lifting my head.

"Exactly," he said, blithely burying the lead. "I'm doubtful you'll go *deaf* deaf."

I didn't want to go any number of deafs.

"It could be worse," he said. "It could be cancer."

This was not the first time Dr. Goldfinger suggested I appreciate my place on the mortality spectrum. I have seen cancer. I'm perfectly aware of the difference between it and everything else. But this is not caveman times. The expression doesn't go: "At least you have some portion of your health." Though I suppose we can't fault our doctors for their skewed view of us. Most of the people with whom they interact have something wrong with them. The patient after me probably came in with his nose in his pocket.

"Okay," I sighed. "What's next?"

"Next we address this empirically."

"Play it by ear, huh?"

He looked pretty disgusted for a man with a literal Rorschach painting in his waiting room.

"First," he explained, "we have to correct the fluid imbalance in your inner ear, which is exacerbating the vertigo. Which means no caffeine and very low salt."

"For how long?"

"For always," he said, "and you'll take a diuretic every day. You'll basically pee all the time."

"Jesus," I said, blinking at him, "could this be any less fun?"

"Maybe lay off the alcohol, too."

* * *

Everyone knows WebMD is a Choose Your Own Adventure book in which all roads lead to death. This did not stop me from doing a "cursory" (hours upon hours) exploration of Ménière's. Alas, I could find little in the way of long-form testimony about it, which has a kind of knock-knock logic: We're all too dizzy to type. But since when does the outside world's lack of interest in medical writing stop people from writing it? Surely I wasn't the only person with a keyboard to be fascinated by my own ailment. I even went on celebritieswithyourdisease.com, which is in desperate need of an editorial director. Under "Mental Illness" there are a mere six names, and one of them is Jean-Claude Van Damme. It would be like finding out the only other person on the planet who shared your birthday was Mandy Moore and trying to extract meaning from that.

Desperate for comrades in affliction, I decided to delve into the Internet's answer to open-mic night: chat forums. Alas, uncommon diseases make for disheartening online experiences. There just aren't enough of us for a quorum. Pleas for assistance are sent up like flares and answered too vaguely (*Have you tried Dramamine?*) or too specifically (*Turns out my TMJ was making it worse, so I got a night guard*). Most suggestions are doled out months after the original cry for help. *Hope you feel better soon!* Soon? What soon? That person has probably fallen off a cliff by now. Then there are the comments with questionable emoji use

(*I've been on the diuretics for a month and now I piss fluorescent* ☺), ones whose targets are misplaced (*I had to give my dog to my boyfriend, who left me for my former "best friend" and now she has my boyfriend* and *my dog. Screw Ménière's!*), or ones that have stumbled into the wrong solar system altogether (*What brand of dust buster does everybody use?*).

The limited promise of comfort was everywhere. It was in the recipes for sodium-free bread (an affront to God's plan), in the links to studies from 1998, in the clip art of cartoon animals conked out and seeing stars. These were uploaded to Facebook by some guy named Gary, who was forced into early retirement by Ménière's. Isolated in his affliction, Gary was probably microwaving a plain baked potato in a condominium somewhere. Maybe Gary and I would not be pals in real life, but we shared a common frailty now.

"I'm sorry you're feeling poorly," I wrote to him. "Hang in there."

Gary never replied. Which was okay. I hadn't given him much to work with. But our lack of correspondence was emblematic of my frustration with the community at large. I'm glad these spaces exist—it's taxing to spend your life explaining your weird illness on top of coping with it. But the more I read, the more put off I became. What I found was not a dialogue but wallowing masquerading as guidance. People driven to write social media posts about their disease have the tendency to treat it like religion or gender, a fundamental tenet of how they want to be categorized. They hashtag their pain. They howl at it without discussing it, without caring much for the response—behavior that would be considered intolerable if they were talking about absolutely anything else. I found myself shame-reading the words of people sicker than I was, cringing at the sad faces that punctuated their sentences. I wanted to distance myself from them because I couldn't distance myself from my own body. No club that would have me as a member, no thank you. It is only in retrospect that I can appreciate the heart of what they were saying: This is who we are now. There is no invisible door for us. We will never break character again.

* * *

That which does not kill us makes us stronger: an idea that started with Nietzsche, got laundered through a century of throw pillows, and came out through the mouth of Kanye West. Suffice to say, Nietzsche didn't actually mean that adversity is the best thing for you. The world's most infamous nihilist was not about to encourage self-betterment. And yet this is exactly what we mean when we say it. It's certainly how Dr. Goldfinger meant it.

He had called to check on my progress (Goldfinger, not Nietzsche). For weeks, I had been eating like a heart patient. I had been sleeping at an angle and hydrating myself into a puddle. I had learned that monitoring one's salt intake is a glimpse into the time-sucking logistics of having an eating disorder. Your hours are spent either thinking about food or purposefully not thinking about food. There is no safe restaurant in which to let loose and order what you want, no designated low-sodium section of any health food store. Products are scattered willy-nilly. You just have to study the nutritional information of everything you touch, as if buying a box of cookies is the biggest decision of your life.

"You'll get used to it," Dr. Goldfinger assured me, as if I had a choice.

This was not some exotic destination that I would one day leave and report back on. This was my home now. But I would adapt the same way one adapts to a new country, to new customs, to new consequences of new laws. Given enough time, the drama drains, the days even out, and life resumes again.

I heard drilling on the other end of the line.

"What is that?" I asked.

"Oh," Dr. Goldfinger said, "there's construction in the hall-way. I don't even hear it anymore."

Then it was two months.

One afternoon, I felt brave enough to take a walk. As I bent down to tie my shoes, I froze. Something was different. Something had gone dormant. I stood up gradually, feeling the joy of stillness shoot through my nerves, afraid to scare it off. Then I went on a bending rampage. I picked things up and put them back down. I sat on all the furniture, marking my territory. I lay on my bed with my head hanging over the edge and flailed around like someone being exorcised. I moved to my desk chair and pretended someone behind me had just called my name. And here, I surprised myself. I did not take it for granted. I did not forget. I stood up and twirled around the living room like they do in the movies, and when I stopped, the world stopped with me.

Wolf

FIRST, I BLAME MY PHONE. MY E-MAIL IS COMING IN BUT NOT going out and such glitches can generally be attributed to one's phone. And to the vaguely mystical forces that exist in order to show us how terrible it is to check e-mail in bed first thing in the morning. But after minutes of pawing at settings, I notice my website isn't working either. So I call up GoDaddy, to see what the trouble is. Like most people, I have limited interaction with my domain host. They are like the DMV or real estate brokers, who become, for brief and tedious moments, a part of your life. But as much as I have not felt compelled to check in with them, they have felt compelled to check in with me. For weeks, they have been trying to reach me via a Hotmail account that I let go to seed years ago. Unable to bill a canceled credit card, they e-mailed again and again, each time expecting a different result—which is the colloquial definition of insanity but okay. Now my name itself, my license plate since the inconvenient days of childhood, has been put up for auction.

"No problem," I tell the customer service representative, demonstrating a staggering mix of denial and ease, "just take it down."

This strikes me as a no-brainer. Perhaps this belies a lack of self-confidence, but how many people are lined up for sloane crosley.com? I've always thought of personal domain names as sentimental objects, of value to precisely one person.

"We don't have it anymore," says the customer service rep.

"Well, who does?"

"That depends."

Am I supposed to guess? What am I, a wizard?

It turns out a person or entity, a noun of some kind, has already purchased the site. No small part of me is amused by the idea of anyone acquiring my website. Apparently, I am the kind of person who would see getting burglarized as a reflection of the quality of her belongings first and as an invasion second. But my comprehension of the situation is still loading. I ask the same question—Wait, what happened?—over and over, thinking this guy is withholding the solution. Now who's colloquially insane?

Unsure of how to further assist me, he transfers me to GoDaddy's domain brokerage department, where a fellow named Adam gives it to me straight. Right now, my domain is being reassigned to the new owner and, while said owner's information should be readily available, it isn't. The Internet is still churning.

I inform Adam that I've intermittently been able to crack into my e-mail, which shocks him as much as it does not shock me. My identity doesn't want to let go of me any more than I want to let go of it.

"This is how it will work," Adam continues. "I will make contact with the new owner and negotiate the best price possible. Usually it's a few hundred dollars but it varies. You would pay that plus a twenty percent commission."

I have questions. Setting aside the eye twitching I experience at alien terminology like "make contact," how is Adam incentivized to negotiate on my behalf if he's getting a commission?

"If it makes you feel any better," he says, "*I'm* not getting the money."

It does not make me feel better. Adam I like. If I could fix this by putting two hundred bucks in a paper bag and shipping it to a sympathetic man in a call center in Iowa, I would. It's the corporate overlords I have a problem with. GoDaddy is not the only company ever invented. If you miss a payment with Verizon, they hunt you down like an animal. They don't wait it out, tapping SOS into a tin can. And whatever happened to robocalls? And how dare he back me into defending Verizon.

Adam tells me these are solid points (into the suggestion box they go!) but none of them are libelous. My domain has been acquired by a third party through legitimate means. There is nothing GoDaddy can do except help me get it back.

"You're welcome to make contact yourself but—"

"But you wouldn't advise it," I finish his sentence.

Understanding the severity of my problem for the first time, I go into string-pulling mode. This is known as grasping at straws when you have no strings to pull. But surely *something* can be done.

When it comes to customer service, I have a trick I am simultaneously proud and ashamed to share here. Proud because it works, ashamed because it is the behavior of a raving lunatic. If the usual means of contacting a company are not working, if you feel helpless and frustrated and like you would be very rich if only you were paid to repeat your issue to a panoply of departments, this is what you are to do: Go to the company's homepage. Scroll down. See the "newsroom" button? Click on it. Here you will find the contact information of public-relations employees. PR is the one department within any corporation that wants to be contacted—or at least needs to be in case, say, two hundred million gallons of oil oopsie into the Gulf of Mexico. Now send a polite-to-the-point-of-obsequious note, explaining your tale of woe. Really get in there. These people don't know you or how far you'll go. They have no measure of your crazy. No one needs to know you have a full life with almost no cats.

Hear that sound? That's the sound of your name being omitted from a group e-mail that reads "You want to take this one, Nancy?"

Randy, the executive assistant to the CEO, calls me immediately. He explains what I already know to be true, that GoDaddy had been trying to reach me via Hotmail before they gave up. I, in turn, explain that rattling off dates is like listing all the times you rang the doorbell of an abandoned house. For me, this just happened. I'm not saying it did. I messed up. But if Randy can't help me legally, logistically, or financially, he can at least do me the courtesy of acknowledging my reality.

"I don't check Hotmail," I say for the umpteenth time. "I use it as a graveyard."

For some reason, this metaphor strikes at the core of Randy.

"You know," he says, "I think we're similar people. Same approach to life, same habits."

Under normal circumstances, I'd be inclined to think this was some kind of customer service gambit, but Randy does not work in customer service. Pop psychology is above his pay grade. A self-described "glass half full" kind of person, he's just a nice guy with "CEO" at the ass end of his title and the burden of talking to me.

"Our guys are really good," he assures me. "I'm sure you'll get your site back."

That I would not be afforded the opportunity to get my domain back had not occurred to me. I am sliding down the ladder of hope at an alarming speed. This morning, anything less than the reinstatement of my account and an apology for the inconvenience would have been unthinkable. Now I am praying for the privilege to send a stranger a piñata full of money. Never outside the realm of fiction have I so deeply fantasized about someone I didn't know and had not seen. Never have I so desperately wanted to breach the barrier of unknowability to understand why a person was not responding to his or her e-mail. Never has my brain been host to the thought: It's just the one planet. How hard could this be?

At 10:30 p.m., like a flashlight dying in a cave, my e-mail goes down for good, refusing to accept my password, which is an elaborate version of a password I've used since college. This feels a little like one's in-box getting sudden-onset dementia. Don't take it personally, you think. This isn't you. This isn't us.

I check the domain registration again. I am now property of a man named Al Perkins.

* * *

British Man Defends Buying B.C. Town Name and Turning It into Porn Site.

According to an article in the Canadian *National Post,* Al Perkins of the British dependency of Jersey recently nabbed the town of Barriere's website and attempted to milk them for $9,700. This will turn out to be only partially true. Perkins does not actually reside on the island of Jersey, only registers his domains there, and Al is not his real name. But the unfortunate part—the milking part—checks out. When the town refused to pay, Perkins raised the stakes and flooded its site with pornography. Which is how visitors to barrierechamber.com wound up "greeted by a wall of explicit images in categories such as 'college,' 'fantasy,' and 'gagging.'"

Well, that does not sound promising.

Technically, what Perkins is doing is legal. He owns the site, he can do what he likes with it, including redirect it. Though this is a seriously disproportionate response to a clerical error. Perkins's defense is that if a domain means that much to someone, why wouldn't he or she renew it? At first, I am struck by how nicely this argument dovetails with my own guilt. How could I have been so negligent? On the other hand, this is the philosophical equivalent of asking, "Why are you hitting yourself?" while slapping someone in the face with their own hand. I maintain my site. And I do so knowing absolutely no one is on the hunt for a 2006 rant about frozen yogurt. Unless I've committed a minor felony, traffic hovers at around eighty visitors per day, two of whom are most definitely my parents. But at least it's mine. Was mine.

I assume barrierechamber.com will be dead—the town has moved on to the more literal pastures of barrierechamberof commerce.com. Instead, it leads me to the Facebook page of one Wesley Perkins. This is surprising, as I gather most people in his line of work do not want to be found. And yet there he is, in his mid-forties with squinty blue eyes and sandy hair. There is something of the elfin Conan O'Brien about him. He is in a relationship with a pretty raven-haired woman named Lesley. There are pictures of their faces pressed close together. Wesley and Lesley. I wonder what Perkins would look like to the unbiased eye. He looks nice. Normal even. Under different circumstances, would I register his smile as an expression of joy and not the cackling of someone who probably cut his teeth stealing wallets from old ladies?

Reasonably, I know the profile of my buyer is irrelevant. It doesn't matter how many puppies this man has skinned. But perhaps this information can be used to manipulate him in some abstract fashion. So I decide to update Adam. He, too, has seen the identity of my domain's new owner. I ask if he's dealt with "them" before. (Perkins is always "they" or "them." This is domain grammar, shorthand for "I don't know how many of who are doing what where.") And yes, Adam has dealt with they. And no, he doesn't sound pleased about having to do so again. I ask him if he's aware that they has a sideline as an amateur pornography peddler who terrorizes Canadians.

"That I did not know," he says.

What Adam does know is that we can expect an initial offer

in the thousands. Oh, how high will we go, how far will we fall? And at what point am I no longer in the business of subsidizing a stranger? I don't bother asking "now what?" because I know "now what." Now we wait.

At 1:02 p.m. the next day, my phone rings. It's my mother. I curse her name and send her to voice mail. At 1:04, the phone rings again. It's Adam. They wants $8,700.

"Fuck they!" I scream into his ear. "Sorry, not you."

"You can cuss all you want," he says. "I'm just not allowed to."

"But you kind of want to, don't you?"

"He's asking for a lot," Adam concedes.

The pronoun is as much of a meltdown as I'm going to get. Over the next few hours, we start trading numbers with Perkins. Us: $1,000. Him: $5,000. Us: $3,200. Him: $4,800. I get the Potemkin-style impression of math being done.

"These numbers are so arbitrary," I whisper.

I have come to the gym to blow off steam. I nearly slid off the treadmill when Adam called. Now I am speaking to him in the open stairwell, agitated but trying to keep my voice down. Between lulls of acceptance I have bouts of revolt. We're talking about four years' worth of electric bills. A trip to Borneo. Thirteen good cashmere sweaters. Twelve hundred cups of coffee.

A woman in a unitard dismounts an elliptical machine and asks me to be quiet.

"I'm sorry," I say, covering the speaker, "it's an emergency."

"I'm trying to work out," she says, pointing at the elliptical machine so I know where it is.

I came here to sweat out my anger. I don't see why she can't do the same. Also, who doesn't bring headphones to the gym? I am about to respond to her—my usual reserves of annoyance are being employed elsewhere but I'm sure I can muster up something for the occasion—when she points at the ground.

"You dropped something," she says.

I look down to see the credit card I had lost. I must have left it in my gym shorts the last time I wore them. I canceled the credit card in December. It's now February. So not only am I at fault for letting my digital self go, but I am at fault for letting my actual self go. I wince, tell Adam to offer $3,500, and hang up the phone.

Meanwhile, my existence has been completely colonized by Perkins. Competing distractions and obligations have been minimized as if on a screen. The only icon left is Perkins's face. The face of a man who, in a sane world, should give no thought to my existence beyond the occasional humbling sense we all get when looking up at the stars or learning about major cities in China. But he has forcibly bound us together. So I find out everything I can. Which, as it turns out, is a lot.

A night of reconnaissance reveals multiple complaints leveled against Perkins via the World Intellectual Property Organization. WIPO is appointed by ICANN, the Internet Corporation for Assigned Names and Numbers. As fabricated and intergalactic as these organizations sound, they're the only recourse for people in my situation. The Internet doesn't have borders. If your identity gets usurped by someone in a foreign country, there's not a ton you can do about it. In an effort to address this issue while simultaneously creating more acronyms, WIPO uses a Uniform Domain-Name Dispute-Resolution Policy (UDRP) for issues "arising from alleged abusive registrations of domain names." Yet even this is not ideal. It takes eight months to resolve a case, for a minimum fee of $1,500. But apparently Perkins is worth it.

One complaint is of particular interest to me. It was filed by a woman named A. D. Justice, who writes novels about men who work for a security company. The covers feature bare-chested hunks with mystifying muscle groups. She doesn't have a trademark but she might as well. Her domain is "the identifier of her work." After redirecting it to a porn site, Perkins offered to sell it back to her for the bargain price of $6,700. But her mama didn't name her "Justice" for nothing. An ICANN panel transferred her domain back to her after finding Perkins's actions to be "indicative of bad faith," a phrase I hope to incorporate more in my daily life. *I notice you've asked me to accompany you to a wedding on the day of the wedding and I find your actions indicative of bad faith. Good day to you, sir!*

If it were just my website at stake, I would follow her lead. I have a middle initial and I am prepared to deploy it. I also work freelance, which means I have no problem squeezing in a vengeance project. But Perkins is also in possession of my primary e-mail address. On the surface, this is no great prize—GoDaddy's e-mail interface is a notch under medieval—but it happens to be host to the majority of my life's correspondence. I don't have time for the law.

At long last, Perkins appears again, demanding $4,200. I pay it. Amex texts me a fraud alert. Because even the robots know something is wrong. But as my confirmation whooshes through the phone, I feel relief. Granted, it's the relief of a man trapped between a boulder and a canyon wall who has decided to chop his own arm off. My options were whittled down but there is control to be had in choosing one. Alas, this feeling is fleeting. Something bad has happened. No one has died. I am not injured or unemployed. I made a mistake and paid for it by wrestling with a pig. Not only did the pig like it, the pig has moved on to other troughs. But I have not.

I pull up the screenshot I took of Perkins's contact information. I know I should delete it. I have paid for two services for the price of one—to get my name back and to get him out of my life. But I find the second benefit unsatisfying. It feels as if, on top of everything else, he took the last word.

Before I can talk myself out of it, I write to him. I explain that I would like to meet him and promise that I am not a nut, come to demand her money back. I just want to ask him a few questions about his business. As he's perfectly aware, I am a writer. And as I am perfectly aware, he is a walking series of transactions with human skin stretched over them. I reason that I just paid him $4,200 to sit down with me. He writes back a few hours later, his name appearing in my newly recovered in-box. He addresses me by my first name, which makes sense. For a hot minute, he was me. He is amenable to chatting but, before we go any further, I should know it's "just business" and I shouldn't "take it personal." He closes with "kind regards." No name beneath. The regards are just floating there, a sentiment sent from no one.

* * *

I have two weeks before I fly to London, where Perkins has agreed to meet me. In this time, we speak once. He is monosyllabic at first, emitting the occasional Cockney "yeah," but once he gets going, he speaks with great enthusiasm about his work. He can't seem to decide if he should brag about his achievements or treat me as suspect for asking. He wants me to know how lucky I am to be speaking with him. He feels at a disadvantage that I know what he looks like but he doesn't know what I look like, so he finds images of me online and chastises me for looking different in some photos than I do in others. I have no explanation for this. A few minutes later, he has a revelation that it's the glasses. Sometimes I'm wearing them and sometimes I'm not.

After the call, he e-mails regularly, wanting to know how many of me are coming, if I'll be "chaperoned." Chances are I'll be coming by private plane on account of me being a writer. He vacillates between helpful and unresponsive. Most missives are peppered with "lol"s. He becomes fixated on the idea that I follow him on Twitter and insinuates that he won't meet me unless I do. At one point, he casually refers to himself as the "wolf of the dot-com." He's not serious . . . but he's a little serious.

It's becoming clear I have no idea who I'm dealing with—but I know who does.

A. D. Justice's real name is Angel Burrage. Turns out her mama didn't name her "Justice," period. She lives in a small town in northwest Georgia and has a voice meant to be threaded into a pillow. And she's happy to chat with a stranger about what happened to her. Unlike me, she did read GoDaddy's renewal e-mails. But she was in the midst of switching over from an old Wordpress site and associated the warnings with property she wanted to lose anyway. So she sat back and did nothing.

"When I realized what happened, I e-mailed him, thinking any normal human being would say, 'Oh, I didn't realize,' and sell it back to me for whatever he paid for it. But that's not what he asked for."

When Angel didn't immediately respond to Perkins's offer, he initiated another conversation, bluntly laying out her choices: not buy the domain, hire a lawyer, or just buy it back from him now. She reasoned she would rather "pay someone to take it away from him than give him a cent." But before she could state her position, she received another message: "Too late. This is no longer for sale."

"He was a real jerk about it," she says. "In one of his e-mails, he wrote, 'It's not like you're a bestseller or anything.'"

"Oh no, he didn't."

"He did. He was fishing for me to object so he could ask for more money. The whole thing was devastating. I was angry at myself for not understanding the process and with him for fully understanding it. I really wanted to track him down, you know?"

I do know. And it's nice to hear my impulses echoed back to me, as everyone in my life has reacted like I'm running toward a burning building.

"It's just hurtful," she says. "All of a sudden I could see everything I had worked to build being flushed away. I felt so violated."

The word sits heavy in my ears. *Violated*. I had not yet identified the feeling myself, but while negotiating with Perkins I was anxious and sleepless and absolutely convinced I was going to get hit by a car. At one point, my neighbor came up behind me as I was putting my key in our door and I spun around, ready to push him off the stoop.

For some people, specifically creative professionals, an eponymous website is not just another avatar—it's the real-time representation of their life's work. *Come, feast your eyes on the output that I hath scraped together between the walls of my dwelling!* Or, as Angel puts it: "I didn't so much feel stolen from. I felt as if someone had stolen me." Unfortunately, these same people are not known for their logistical prowess. A website is often their sole foray into the tech world, the second-most administrative thing they do after refilling a stapler. They build these shrines to self out of necessity so that they can get back to work out of greater necessity.

Angel thinks I won't get an iota of remorse out of Perkins. When she says it, I feel so silly for fantasizing that I might get it that I deny I want it and then feel bad all over again for denying it. Maybe I really do need to talk this out. So I ask around, trying to find more people who have had this happen to them, a makeshift support group for the domainishly challenged. A few friends have had to pay a hundred dollars for a lost domain here and there. Speeding ticket money. Nothing to write home about. Except for my friend Kenji Bunch. Kenji is a violist in Portland, Oregon. He is in possession of all his credit cards, but his descent into the underbelly of the Internet began with him switching contact e-mails and forgetting to inform his registrar. Before he knew it, his name was sold at auction to a Chinese domainer named Heng Zhong.

"I guess I could have just switched to dot-org but dot-org felt a little grandiose. Like I'm on a mission to help all the Kenji Bunches in the world. I felt like my best shot was to try to appeal to this guy's humanity."

Kenji forwards me his eloquent plea to Heng Zhong, who suggests $5,000 as an appropriate bounty. Like Perkins, Zhong refers to his "business" and to Kenji as someone who has willingly entered this exchange. I've noticed domainers often speak of "transactions" made and "deals" closed. This would be as adorable as a child pretending to have a tea party if the tea weren't laced with arsenic. By Zhong's logic, Kenji is at fault not only for letting his domain lapse but for undervaluing it with a low bid. Zhong also accuses him of having a "bad personality" and "something wrong with his brain." Though this is somewhat understandable, given Kenji's assertion that he's renamed himself Heng Zhong and gone ahead and registered www.TheOther HengZhongIsABottomFeedingLowlifeScumLeadingAnEmpty Existence.com.

Kenji suggests I speak to his friend, Daniel Feldeson, a Brooklyn-based composer, who's had a similar experience. The Internet is littered with all kinds of domain horror stories but a healthy amount of them come from singers and guitarists. I am starting to wonder if musicians are somehow even worse at holding down their domains than authors, but this feels like rubbing salt in the wound.

"I was righteously indignant and deeply annoyed," Daniel says, "just like you."

Well, almost. The difference between Angel and Kenji and me and Daniel is that Daniel doesn't feel this way toward the stranger who demanded $2,000 for his site—but toward GoDaddy.

"I felt like the company had done me this incredible disservice. It felt weird to sell my domain to a pirate when there's really nobody else in the world who'd want it. It's insane. There must be a better way."

There's not. I understand Daniel's feelings, as they are my feelings. If Wesley Perkins can find me, why can't my provider find me first? But barring global regulation of over 64 million sites, GoDaddy's hands are tied. For one thing, their system works like a giant pawnshop. It's uninterested in the origin story of that bloody Rolex. It can't parse the difference between an available domain and a lost domain. For another, they are only complicit inasmuch as they have a department devoted to solving the problem. Companies like GoDaddy scale by removing human interaction, and, as Adam told me, the performance evaluations of the brokerage staff are based on their closure rate. The commission exists because, even if you're in the right, someone has to come in to work and deal with you.

For now, the company has what it refers to as a "grace period." This is the five stages it takes for your domain to die. While you're walking around with this symptom-free but fatal disease, this is what's happening: Between day one and day eighteen of expiration, everything can be reverted back to you without penalty. On day nineteen, your site is technically yours but only for an eighty-dollar redemption fee. A week later, your domain is officially put up for auction. This sounds dire, but you can still get it back, it's just that now you've got a price sticker on your forehead. Ten days after *that* is when things get messy. The domain is listed in a closeout auction, at which point you have a forty-eight-hour window to reclaim your domain, regardless of the winning bid. That is, assuming you magically decided to stop ignoring six weeks of e-mails. But who among us swings by the emergency room for the heck of it? So now you're dead, having graduated from purgatory to the aftermarket. And it is here all manner of ghouls await you.

* * *

Sixteen hours before we're supposed to meet, Perkins pulls the plug. It's unclear if he's joking, but I did not fly 3,500 miles to eat a scone and go home. Not wanting him to know where I'm staying, I call him from my cell phone, which leads him to believe that I couldn't possibly be in London. Once assured that I am, he expresses newfound concern that if I write about this, he will not be "painted in a positive light." This, despite weeks of claiming he has never and will never care what people think of him. His concerns are not unfounded. But I tell him if he's worried his job description will reflect poorly on him, he has bigger problems than me. I'm simply curious to know who he is and why he does this. Which, as it turns out, is the truth.

Perkins has begun exhibiting curious signs of humanity. He's told me the story of the single mother who once called him, sobbing and destitute, so he gave her back her site on the spot. He says he chose to meet in London over his native Birmingham because there's more for me to see here. He's assigned himself the role of research assistant, suggesting people for me to talk to, cases to look up. He's even sent me random closeout auction domains so that I can "save them from my same fate." Among them are a country singer, a third-generation heating and cooling business, a wellness author, and a domestic-abuse hotline. He would call himself but he "sounds too much like a scammer" to be believed.

"So you've done this before?" I asked. "Tracked people down?"

"'Course I have."

Now, as I pace and cajole, he wants to know how my "savior mission" went. I report that some people were grateful—though only moderately so, as it's hard to grasp the emotional and financial consequences of letting your domain expire until it happens—and some never responded. Perhaps because "an urgent message regarding your domain" sounds about as unurgent as messages come. Or the timing was farcically bad. The heating and cooling company's Web designer was on a cruise in the middle of the Atlantic. With the country singer, I wrote to his manager and his agent, to no avail. I tried to get to him through his Twitter profile, only to find a "Hey guys, taking a break from social media. Mental health!"

"You see?" Perkins asks, almost gleefully. "You get it now. Even if you're trying to be a Good Samaritan, half the time it doesn't work anyway."

* * *

A pipe has burst in the pub Perkins selected, so we agree to meet outside. He is his profile picture come to life—forty-six, five nine, compact and quick-gestured. He grins when he spots me, an open smile that pokes into his cheeks. Yesterday's trepidations seem to have melted away. He greets me warmly, kissing me on the cheek. He wants to make sure I accurately describe what he's wearing: "I got on brand boots, slim-fit jeans, a muscle-fit T-shirt. Athletic build, would you say?" We proceed to speed-weave through the streets of Marylebone, a neighborhood with which he's only marginally familiar, but Lesley wanted to do some shopping here (sexist but inevitable thought: her and whose money?). He's concerned that another pub will be too loud. So we settle on a café, which is fine by Perkins because he doesn't drink.

"If you hear my phone bleeping," he warns me, "I'm bidding on domains."

He winks. My face contorts like a baby's, practicing amusement. I have never reminisced with someone about the time they took my money and my identity. He orders a soda and thanks me for earning him an unexpected $4,800 yesterday. What $4,800? I am as confused as he wants me to be. Apparently, while we spoke on the phone last night, Perkins was in the midst of negotiations. Panicked by the silence, the domain's rightful owner increased his bid to meet Perkins's asking price.

"So really I have to thank you, Sloane. You did that."

My stomach turns. Perkins's second-favorite activity after domain acquisition is needling me. (When I informed him that I'd be staying with a friend, I got a "You have friends?" in return.) He seems to be waiting for a "You're welcome." I change the subject. Perkins is self-taught, having stumbled into his current revenue stream by accident four years ago. He's an "online trader" and was looking for an expired domain for himself, one that had some traffic already, when he came across unitedfinancial.org. He bought it, but it turned out the credit union wanted it back. So Perkins sold it to them for a cool $15,000.

"That's still the highest domain sale I ever done. I tend to keep it just under 10K. It's sort of like psychology. I've found that if you keep it under 10K, it gives people hope. So if you give 'em a carrot at 9.7K, yeah? They think they can get it at 5K. And if we do a deal at 5K, I'm happy because I've only paid a few hundred and they're happy because they've gotten a good price."

I search my memory for a time I've felt "happy" since this happened. Nope. Nothing.

Soon Perkins was trolling auction sites for nearly expired domains. He prefers fishing for preexisting domains over squatting on ones he suspects might be valuable, so he set the parameters for an algorithm to do just that. Perkins has a nemesis in the form of a domainer in LA called Scarface ("Me and him hammer away at it all the time"). He's written Scarface in the hopes of teaming up since they're costing each other thousands of dollars a year but Scarface is a lone wolf. No matter, Perkins knows his algorithm is better. It doesn't just search for traffic, but for the status of a site, organic traffic, and, most crucially, the duration of ownership. Perkins claims not to target individuals, but his algorithm is a heat-seeking missile for personal domains. We look like what we are—people who have lost something and will want it back. By his own admission, celebrities and corporations "tend to have enough people looking that someone always warns 'em before I get there."

"Your problem," he concludes, "is that you're not more famous."

"Yes, that's definitely my problem."

"And what the hell were you using Hotmail for? You deserve to lose your site just for that."

Perkins slaps the table and laughs. He may have the moral center of a Cadbury Creme Egg but he's also starting to sound like every single one of my friends.

"You just gotta ask yourself," he levels with me, "how do you value your brand? Some people think no, I'm not giving him the money, because they want to make a stance, but the stance can harm their business. And hey, I lose a lot. Sometimes I'm buying twenty domains at a time and spending two thousand dollars, yeah? It's like being in a casino. You know when your number drops in and you're like 'Yes!'? That's what it feels like. But what happens if I don't sell anything? You start to get on the brink. It's highly risky."

Perkins sees himself as a casualty of his chosen profession, which is a bit like a cat burglar becoming irate because he threw out his back scaling your building. But this is the reasoning required to do his job. He loses money. He gets threatened. People have vowed to hunt him down and cut his throat. Even so, I can tell that it takes such extremes for him to register contact as anything but further proof that humanity is divided into chumps and not chumps. There are countless ways to divide the world in two. Gender, religion, nut allergies. But Perkins does some of the more cynical line-drawing I've ever witnessed. When I tell him as much, he says he doesn't see it that way. Not at all. In fact, he thinks he's providing a service.

"Listen," he says, leaning in close. "The domain could end up in someone's hands who's bad. Some of these mega-rich domainers, they won't even sell you the domain back, yeah? They use it for traffic or adverts. At least I'm giving people the opportunity to buy it back."

This steal-from-the-rich, sell-to-the-poor policy ebbs and flows. Perkins cops to the real reason he sometimes contacts domain owners at the last minute—and it's not because he's trying to be an upstanding citizen. It's because he "got carried away" in an auction and would rather those people purchased their sites back before he has to pay for them. I am visibly disappointed but, as Perkins points out, the calculus cuts both ways. The real reason he redirects personal sites to pornographic ones is not so nefarious as it seems. It's so he can turn a profit while he waits for the original owner to pony up the cash. And should the flashes of asses expedite the process? All the better.

Plus, as he is quick to remind me, it's all perfectly legal. I posit the idea that legality and morality don't always overlap. There are a lot of bad things in this world that are perfectly legal. Laws are created by man and man is fallible. He shrugs. He has my money and I don't so he's more or less done with this particular debate.

"The interesting thing," he muses, "is there seems to be a lot of personal sites now. A lot of what I call 'love me's. You know, the girls who love themselves and it's all 'I'm this, I'm that, blah blah blah,' because they watch too much TV and they get caught up in their own lives and they all think they're Kim Kardashian."

I know exactly of what he speaks, having screenshotted an Instagram feed or two in my time and texted it to a like-minded friend. But I am unwilling to turn my back on my own gender in his presence. Perkins concedes that there are exceptions to the rule. Like his own daughter, a college student with her own lifestyle and fashion site. He set it up for her—and nearly let it expire.

"Can you believe it? Bad! I know. But I have thousands of 'em."

"Does she know what you do for a living?"

"She just knows I do something with domains. The thing you have to understand, yeah? Is that this is all a simple business transaction. I don't do nothing to people. If you value your entire business at five hundred dollars, then it's time to close your doors. It's a self-inflicted lesson."

Talking to Perkins is like talking to a perfectly reasonable person until, only when he turns to the side, you see a little chunk of his head is missing. Because he's not wrong—not a bastion of ethics, but not wrong. He's taking advantage of a deeply flawed system. If you lose a watch and I buy it for cheap at a flea market and then wind up selling it back to you on eBay, well, I can sleep at night knowing I've done that. Chances are I'm not just giving it back. What bothers me is the idea of doing it every day, intentionally combing the world for lost watches until I am an expert watch reseller and, more frighteningly, an expert sleeper. Until people are not people but watches with wrists still in them. I suggest that Perkins could be doing something else with his time— he has an eye for the stock market, a certain charm and, clearly, Web experience—but he shakes his head no. He likes the thrill of this too much. Plus, he thinks he's hungrier for it than most.

"I'm not like these domainer guys who do this who are from rich backgrounds. I'm more from the streets. And I do think other people have more money than me. I mean, take you. You live in New York. Your apartment costs three million dollars."

At this, I can't help but smile. Between him and GoDaddy, I paid over two months' rent to get back something I owned and made. This wasn't a medical expense or an airfare change fee, both infuriating but both the price of living life. In this case, I just set the money on fire. Until I am on the ransom end of an actual hostage situation, this will be the most painful expense I ever have. And let's say I did live in a three-million-dollar apartment.

That wouldn't mean I deserved this. But if there's one business Perkins and I have both willingly entered, it's the business of being an adult. In the end, it is not my place to convince him what he's doing is wrong any more than it's his to convince me that it isn't.

"You think I should feel guilty," he says, as we leave the café. "I never feel guilty. If I was rich, maybe I'd keep the algorithm going and set up a charity and tell all these people to donate to some cause instead of paying me."

He smiles, running a simulation of this alternate future in which he is lauded for what he does. I tell him I'm not sure that would work. People don't donate to charity under duress.

"Oh, trust me," he says, holding the door open, "they would."

Our
Hour
Is
Up

I SOMEHOW MAKE IT TO THE FOURTH GRADE WITHOUT EVER seeing the *Peanuts* comic strip. So I don't know that I'm imitating Lucy when I put signs up all over my elementary school, advertising my services as a therapist. In puffy paint and Magic Marker, I inform my peers that every Tuesday I will station myself on the large rock that dominates the northwest quadrant of the playground and anyone who likes can come and ask me for advice. I know what you're thinking: Why Tuesdays? Because Monday is too loaded, Friday is not loaded enough, Thursday is charged with anticipation for Friday, and Tuesday is essentially a less popular version of Wednesday. And "less popular" is exactly where I belong.

There are kids who go through elementary school having no friends whatsoever. But between parent and teacher pressure for harmony, this is actually tough to manage. It generally requires hygiene issues or the regular cutting of one's own bangs. I am the kid just above that rung, the one with a handful of friends. Scraped together, there are just enough of them for me to suspect that if they have sought my nine-year-old wisdom at bowling parties, perhaps I can be of use to the population at large. Because I have the brain of a small child, it does not occur to me to charge for this service.

The Monday before I open this not-for-profit juggernaut, I am pulled out of class by the principal. This is beyond shocking to everyone, including the teacher, including me. At this point in my life, my greatest infraction has been forgetting my recorder on a school bus. My heart races as I try to imagine what I could possibly have done.

It seems that I did not have permission to tape posters up all over the place, and if I had asked, I would have been informed that the entire school had just been freshly repainted. Now there are bits of colored construction paper embedded in the walls. It will be years before I do the calculus on how much it costs to repaint an entire public school and where that money comes from. For now, it doesn't seem like a very big deal. Perhaps the principal should bore someone else with her list of chores. I apologize but my real concern is that my therapeutic practice is getting off to an inauspicious start.

The good news is that word has spread that I was pulled out of

class and why. This is the moment in which I learn that all publicity is good publicity. Or, well, I learn the adage. On Tuesday,
when the lunch bell rings, I march past the tire swings and the
monkey bars and climb up onto the rock like a Buddha in a jean
jacket. At first, business is slow. It's just me and my best pal, chatting. She is the human equivalent of the pianist's own money in
the tip jar. But soon enough, people we don't know as well come
around and she excuses herself to apply stickers to her backpack.

During my first recess, I have four customers. Their problems
stem mostly from one another. One day, licensed therapists will
tell them that their problems stem mostly from their parents, but
that day has not yet come. For now, it's all Suzy-is-mean-to-me
and Danny-stole-my-gummy-bears. There's a fifth customer, at the
end of the hour, but he only asks me a question about the dearth
of strawberry milk in the cafeteria. I can't decide if he doesn't
understand what I'm doing here or I don't.

A few Tuesdays into this enterprise, Jason Pakarinen leaves the
enclosure around the basketball court and saunters up the concrete path that leads to my rock. I think he will turn off at any
minute because Jason Pakarinen couldn't possibly be coming
to talk to me. I am not disgusted by boys like some of my friends.
I am, in fact, madly in love with Jason Pakarinen. His mother
and my mother are quite friendly, but this has never stopped him
from pretending I don't exist. The fact that Jason Pakarinen even
has a mother is bewildering to me. What does one make a perfect
boy for dinner? How does one tell him what to do? What does he
dream of at night?

This is really happening. Jason Pakarinen is headed straight
toward me. My clientele is expanding in marvelous directions.

"Yeah," Jason Pakarinen begins.

This speaks to the intimate secrets he's about to reveal—he greets me as if we've been conversing for hours.

"Yeah, I have a problem," he says.

Dear God, I think, has he prepared a speech?

"Yes?" I ask, fluttering my nascent eyelashes. "How can I help you, Jason?"

"Yeah, there's this really annoying girl giving advice on a rock."

To his credit, this is a pretty sick burn for a fourth grader. I make a mask of my face as if unaffected, even though I am desperate to dispose of my own body.

"What do you think I should do about it?" he asks, round-house kicking my feelings.

"Shut up," I tell him.

I mean it as a jab but it comes out as more of a guess. *Shut up* and *boner* occupy the deepest crevices of my insult bag. I have to dust them off before deploying them.

Jason Pakarinen laughs—cackles, really—and walks away. I watch him intently to see if he's returning to his friends. Much to my relief, he's headed for the boys' room. Alas, this means that my humiliation was but an errand for him. He had to pee the whole time.

* * *

Twenty years later, I am standing behind a police barricade on Fifth Avenue because it's the Gay Pride parade and all parades are awful at the molecular level, even ones for clean air and kittens. I am with my boyfriend and we are waiting for our turn to cross the street. We've been standing here for so long, I can't remember a time before we were standing here. There's so much cheering and stimulation that it takes an adult Jason Pakarinen several attempts at calling my name before I hear it.

I turn around to see that he, too, is waiting to cross the street. Because of social media and life in general, I recognize him as instantly as he recognizes me. He's wearing fancy spandex and leaning on a sleek bicycle that looks like a paper clip that fell from heaven. If there were any justice in the world, Jason Pakarinen would be drinking in an Applebee's in the middle of the day with his ass crack showing. But there is no justice in this world. Jason Pakarinen went on to be well-liked throughout high school and graduated from Stanford and a bunch of other schools and is currently a physicist in London.

Who let him back into the country?

We embrace. Because apparently, being an adult is about the same thing as being in fourth grade: embracing your sworn enemy. I admonish myself for being flattered that Jason Pakarinen is so happy to see me. I introduce him to my boyfriend and they chat about total nonsense. Like the pros and cons of dropping off one's laundry. I am gobsmacked by how they can have such a dull conversation, as if the universe didn't just collapse on itself. But it does make me happy to imagine a little girl such as myself, wondering what my boyfriend ate for dinner when he was a kid, knowing he was not a cruel child.

When a cop moves the barricade aside, we all hustle through

together. Jason Pakarinen tells us all about his life, about how wonderful London is and how he's just gut renovated a house for himself and his wife, a pickle monger who's pregnant with twins.

"They're mine," he says, making a clever joke.

I tell him about a novel I just bought, holding up the bag as proof, as if purchasing a novel trumps everything he has just said. My boyfriend, who never knew Jason Pakarinen, the boy-god, looks at me like I've been drinking. At the end of the block, I assume Jason Pakarinen and his bike will cut into the park, but he keeps following us, wheeling and talking.

"I'm so glad I ran into you," he says.

Again, I try not to be flattered. Finally, as we reach another corner, he shows his cards. His mother heard from my mother that I used to work at a publishing house.

"This is true," I tell him.

"My wife is putting together a book proposal," he says.

"On pickle mongering?" asks my boyfriend.

"She's really popular in the UK," explains Jason Pakarinen. "I wonder if I can ask you to look at the book proposal."

"I worked in publicity," I explain. "I didn't really see proposals."

I have seen hundreds upon hundreds of book proposals.

"Oh," says Jason Pakarinen.

I can tell he's about to give it another go. You don't get into Stanford by giving up that easy!

"Well," he says, "maybe if you just had any advice for her . . . I'll e-mail you."

"I rarely check it," I say. "Anyway, it was nice to bump into you!"

I give him a hug so brief it could pass for a breeze, grab my boyfriend, and pull him away. In my peripheral vision, I see Jason Pakarinen looking confused, as if he has overstepped his bounds. And maybe he has. I don't ask people I haven't seen in twenty years for favors. I don't go up to doctors at parties and ask them to look at a weird bump on my thumb, and I certainly don't say, "Wait here, I want you to look at my wife's weird thumb bump." As far as Jason Pakarinen is concerned, my advice-giving days are over. Shop's closed. But perhaps this doesn't justify physically running from this blast from the past as if a shard had hit me in the eye.

"Well, that was a little on the bitchy side," my boyfriend decides.

I know it was. But I give him a dirty look for saying it first. He is undeterred, waiting for an explanation for this incongruous behavior. What he does not realize is that it's not incongruous—it's overdue. What he does not realize is that Jason Pakarinen is responsible for a fragment of the woman he loves, a fragment so small no one would notice it missing but me. I look over my shoulder to make sure that Jason Pakarinen has disappeared. Then I ask him who his favorite *Peanuts* character was and cross my fingers for the right answer.

The
Doctor
Is
a
Woman

I USED TO SUBSCRIBE TO A MAGAZINE THAT CAME WITH A POST-card crammed in the spine of each issue. On one side of the postcard was a famous work of art, on the other a thin line, split-ting the negative space. Standard postcard protocol. I liked the postcards mostly because I like to avoid clutter and they gave me something to throw out. Except for one. A photograph of a tent called *Everyone I Have Ever Slept With*, by the British artist Tracey Emin. Inside a camping tent, Emin had stitched the names of anyone she'd ever shared a bed with, from friends to relatives to lovers. The tent's reproduction on a postcard whittled its mean-ing down to the provocative title, but that was enough to save it from the trash. I put it on the mantel of my defunct fireplace, where I kept other precious keepsakes, like crumpled receipts, votive candles, and free-floating sticks of gum.

One night, as I was making dinner, I smelled something burning in the living room. Somehow the postcard had migrated near one of the lit candles and begun to smoke. I rushed to blow it out, thinking only of the vulnerability of my own belongings. But the next morning, on the cover of the arts section of *The New York Times*, was the headline *London Warehouse Fire Destroys Artworks*. At 2 a.m., right around when my postcard went up in flames in New York, a fire blew through a warehouse in east London, destroying millions of dollars' worth of artwork, including the tent. I couldn't believe my eyes but then, in an instant, I could. An instant is how long it takes to convince yourself of anything—that a banging shutter is an intruder, that you could live off juice for a week, or, in my case, that I was a full-blown witch.

In the wake of my latent powers, I looked into seeing a psychic. Game recognize game and all that. I had never been to a psychic before. I figured if I want to throw my money away, I'd be better served buying six-dollar lattes. Or curling up cash into little tubes and shoving it down the drain. As far as I'm concerned, the psychics on the sidewalk are hucksters: the ones with the neon signs tell you what you want to hear and the good ones tell you what you already know. *You have a fraught relationship with your mother.* Oh, do I? Go on. They're also notoriously poor marketers. Once I walked past a door that read PSYCHIC WITHIN, which I took to mean "within me" and kept walking.

Eventually, I settled on a psychic who came recommended by a rational friend whose only point of earthly disconnect was a nonsensical aversion to gluten. She sold me on this guy using the one guaranteed pressure point for any skeptic: our own skepticism. How could I be sure that my conception of the universe is the absolute one? I could not. Technically, this fellow was an "intuitor," which I found less hubristic than "psychic." And he had an actual office, which was encouraging. The office was located in a building in the Flatiron, behind a wavy glass door. Gold lettering on the door read PLEASE KNOCK. This was less encouraging. What kind of intuitor requires a knock at the door?

He welcomed me inside, sat me down, dumped a shot of ginger into his tea, and informed me that I would have many children.

"You will have many children," he said.

"Don't you need to see my palm first or something?"

He seemed insulted. He doesn't come to my house and tell me how to turn the computer on.

"No," he said, shuffling a pack of tarot cards.

When I told him about the postcard, he was unimpressed. For me, it was one of the crazier things that had ever happened, one of the few life events that did not fall under the purview of coincidence. I was like one of those out-of-control mutant school brats. For him, it was as if I wanted a parade for flushing the toilet.

"You are not a destroyer," he assured me, trying to rid me of an idea that had never occurred to me. "Energy is like a giant sweater. All you did was tug on a thread. And by doing that, you have created something."

"I know," I agreed. "A five-alarm fire."

"No," he said, "not that."

There were tiny bells sewn into the seam of his head scarf. They chimed as he shook his head back and forth.

"You have created the children."

"What children?"

"Yours."

"Whose?"

"Yours."

I looked over my shoulder.

"The children inside you," he clarified, pointing at my belly.

I did not sign up for this Ray Bradbury shit. It's one thing to predict the future, it's quite another to alter its course. How could I possibly have made children, nay, "many children," simply by coming here? If this were feasible, he should change his business cards and become the richest man in America.

"I don't think about children," I said.

This came out chillier than I meant it, like I was snubbing a street canvasser. It's not that I was against children. I was not one of those women who felt the need to stress how much she *never* played with baby dolls as a child. As if the budding embracement of the power to procreate is somehow shameful. You're not one of *those* girls. Not you. It's just that I was still in my early twenties and against participating in a version of my life in which I wound up crediting a stranger for calling my motherhood in advance.

I explained that, as a literate female, it's difficult to control the flow of stories debating the merits of motherhood, pumping women full of anxiety and presumptive regret, yammering on about the inflexibility of biological time if you want to have kids and the inflexibility of actual time after you have them. As if it's entirely in your hands anyway, which it's not if you're single or poor or both. So I had opted to turn the faucet off entirely. Even the articles about how one is permitted to forgo babies only added to the pressure. One or two in isolation, okay. I might have read those. I'm sure they're very good. But there were just too many. The more they screamed about a woman's right to make her own stigma-free decision, the more they kept the topic in circulation. So, at the risk of remaining ill-informed about my own desires and thus engaging in the kind of self-suppression that has haunted women for centuries, I closed my eyes and tried to think of nothing. Sometimes it worked. Other times I saw a giant uterus with fallopian tube arms, terrorizing the city, ripping the crown off the Statue of Liberty before sinking into the Hudson.

"It doesn't matter," the intuitor said. "The children think about you."

Okay, I thought. Good for them. Can we get back to me being a witch?

"They're coming," he stressed.

I told him I didn't want the kind of children who show up to places uninvited. He took a sip of his tea, smiling at me as if I, too, had taken a sip of the tea. Then he shouted:

"And I'm sure your tent didn't want to be set on fire but— poof!"

For this, I gave him sixty dollars and left the building. I briefly wondered if I should tip him. Does one tip an intuitor? A retroactive tipping system might be the way to go. *Tell you what: Turns out I get eaten by that anaconda, there's a ten-dollar bill in an envelope with your name on it.* I waited on line at the coffee shop downstairs. Where was this army of babies going to come from? I had no plans to get artificially inseminated, was bothered by the mere sound of it, and, even if I did, I wasn't going to start that afternoon. At the time, I didn't have a boyfriend or even a guy friend whom I could see as the father of my child, if only he'd take off his glasses and undo his ponytail. The only thing I was expecting was a six-dollar latte.

* * *

Most children are okay once you get to know them. They're like your flakiest, least employable friend who sleeps through brunch, makes terrible art, and name-drops characters you've never heard of. They're also easy to beat at tag. Personally, I like my child friends to be at least seven years old, as there is little difference between what amuses me and what amuses a seven-year-old. But the idea of pushing a whole person through my major organs has always been simultaneously too abstract and too horrible. As someone who has met pregnant women, I can tell you that babies pound your bladder into a pancake and put your stomach level with your heart. This would be funny if women were men because the joke with men is that the way to their hearts is through their stomachs. But women are not men.

Deep down, I thought it was a moot point anyway. I secretly thought that if I ever wanted to become pregnant, a doctor would tell me that my uterus was not broken, but absentee. There's just a bunch of insulation foam where a uterus might go. The one time I had reason to purchase a pregnancy test, I peed on the stick and waited for one blue line or two blue lines. When the timer went off, I went to check on the stick. The window was blank. Like a

Magic 8 Ball without the magic. I consulted the box. "Blank" was not an option. I tried again with a second stick. Same deal. So I called my mother, who is generally useless on such matters but had recently knocked it out of the park after I lamented that a guy I was dating had never heard of Gloria Steinem.

"Eh," she had said, "find out if his mother doesn't know who she is. Then you're really screwed."

I thought perhaps this comment had ushered in a new era of wisdom. I was mistaken.

"This is a good thing," she assured me about the test. "Clearly, you're not pregnant!"

"I'm not 'not pregnant,'" I said. "I'm nothing."

"Which would you rather be?" she asked. "Pregnant or nothing?"

Those were my options? For so much of history, to not be pregnant *was* to be nothing. And while we have mostly sloughed off such beliefs, some animal part of me was speaking up, making a strong case for "pregnant." Another minute passed before a solitary blue line appeared in the window. I sighed, relieved. But we will never know who was the remedial one, me or the stick.

* * *

As I got older, I was surprised to find it was not my fellow women who were pressuring me to have a baby or even to have an opinion. You'd think a group of people who dress for one another would also have babies for one another. Not so. While I'm acquainted with a few status moms who believe what the world

really needs is more Americans, and who ask, "What are you waiting for?" as if I have—whoops!—lost track of time, none of my
actual girlfriends pressed the topic. They knew better. As for the
question of immortality, of pushing my bloodline into the future,
well, this is not the primary preoccupation of my gender.

Yet just about every guy I dated assumed that children were at
the forefront of my brain. They became increasingly vocal about
this, ridding me of my need to ignore the mountain of trend
pieces—they brought the mountain to me. One guy was forever
sniffing out my DNA-hustling agenda. He shoehorned the topic
into conversations about guacamole. *You ever try to put toothpicks
through an avocado pit? If only that's how babies were made!* His
lack of verbal agility hit rock bottom as we lay on the beach one
summer, chatting with our chins resting on our fists. I asked him
if my back was getting red and he asked me what I would do if I
got pregnant.

"What are you going to do if you go bald?" I shot back.

"That's totally different," he said.

"Biologically," I agreed, "not topically."

By this time, I was thirty-four. I told him that I wasn't sure
what I would do. Because I wasn't. Furthermore, I resented what
I perceived to be the weaponization of my own vulnerability for
the purposes of this conversation. I could tell it would have been
preferable if I had sprung to my feet and drawn ABORTIONS 4EVA
in the sand. Looking back, it's clear that he was building a case
for himself, a verbal paper trail in which the reason it didn't
work out with us was because I was in a hurry to procreate.
When the truth was he just wasn't sure he wanted to have kids

with *me*. Which was fair. I wasn't sure I wanted kids with me either.

* * *

There's an old riddle that goes like this: A father and son are in a car accident. The father dies instantly, and the son is taken to the nearest hospital. The doctor comes in and exclaims, "I can't operate on this boy!"

"Why not?" the nurse asks.

"Because he's my son," the doctor replies.

How is this possible?

The riddle is a good litmus test for how we're doing as a society. How quickly does the person being riddled to register that the doctor is a woman? It's hard to imagine a grown individual being confounded by this brain buster—even the language, "nearest," hints that everyone in the riddle has a familiarity with one another—but I remember being stumped by it as a kid. Probably because my coterie of medical advisers consisted of a pediatrician, an allergist, and an orthodontist, all of whom were men. I was too busy cracking my teeth on hard candies, oblivious to the patriarchy.

But even knowing what I know now, I still don't understand the doctor's reaction. I don't get the setup. Why can't a mother operate on her son? Obviously, it's not ideal. Her judgment could be obscured by emotion. Someone else really should do it. But I always picture the riddle taking place in a rural town, where she is the only doctor on duty. I imagine her pacing the hall while her son bleeds out on a gurney. All because she can't pull it to-gether. She just seems like a bad doctor and a hysterical woman, which transforms the riddle from feminist to sexist. Was this lady responsible enough to have a child in the first place? Or did she absorb so many outside opinions that she failed to develop one of her own?

* * *

By thirty-six, I was expending more energy avoiding the topic than it would have taken to address it. Like leaving instructions for houseguests about a "tricky" showerhead when all parties would be better served by a new showerhead. But by ignoring the con-versation, I had put myself in conversation with the conversation. I was tired of maintaining the protective cloak of apathy I had once valued. There's a term for this in economics: *diminishing marginal utility*. It's the only economics term I know and I prob-ably retained it for times like this, for understanding the moment when more of what used to make you happy no longer does.

Which is how I found myself, on an idle Wednesday, at a fer-tility center located high above Columbus Circle. I came in for a general check on my fecundity, a medical morsel to tide me over. Was I broken or not broken? This was not a debate. This was a quiz. I could take a quiz.

I sat in a waiting room with a nice view of Central Park, star-ing at a woman across from me as she knitted a baby blanket. At first, I dismissed this as wearing the band's T-shirt to the show. But as I watched her needles go back and forth, clacking over each other, I became hypnotized. Her pain was so palpable, it was as if the needles were the one thing tethering her to polite society. If she dropped them, she might start screaming. I felt as if I could walk over, press my finger against her forehead, and sit back down. Even as I pitied her, I was jealous. She knew what she wanted and thus had the capacity to be disappointed when she didn't get it. Whereas I was afraid that by the time I knew, there would be nothing to hope for.

More women came in with husbands or partners or mothers, each pair looking more solemn than the last. This whole place was a six-word Hemingway story. The receptionist handed the newly arrived their informational folders. On the cover of the folder were tiny baby pictures arranged to form the face of one giant baby. This struck me not only as a Chuck Close rip-off, but as poor folder design. For patients like me, pictures of babies were intimidating and foreign. For patients like the blanket knitter, pictures of babies should come with a trigger warning. The whole reason I had selected this place to begin with was because their website featured the words *Let us help you meet your family goals* superimposed over a young couple playing with a Labrador. Turns out they lure you in with the promise of puppies right before they stick an ultrasound wand up your vagina.

An ultrasound screen is something you just don't see outside of a doctor's office. You have never owned a TV shaped like the trail of a windshield wiper. So it's no wonder we cross-stitch meaning with the image before us. Ultrasounds are the place where gender makes itself known, where one heartbeat becomes two, where one heartbeat becomes none. It's package tracking for your unborn child. It was therefore unsettling to look at mine and see a wasteland of static. I was a healthy woman who wasn't pregnant, so seeing anything in there, even an extra set of house keys, would have been disturbing. But how strange to look at a live cam of one's own uterus and confront emptiness.

The technician left me in the dark as I got dressed. I felt a hollow ball of grief expand in my body, but I couldn't say what for. I couldn't even say if it was real. Should I cry at the frozen tundra of my insides? Where had I put my underwear?

After the exam, I sat across from the fertility doctor in her office while, stone-faced, she reviewed my test results. On the doctor's desk were three glass sculptures, each with a colored jellyfish blown into the center.

"Those are funny," I said.

"Oh," the doctor deadpanned, "they were a gift."

Their bright tentacles so clearly resembled fallopian tubes; I was sad for this woman who surrounded herself by people who had failed to point this out to her. She closed my chart. Then she began explaining the reproductive process from scratch. As in from conception. I nodded the way I nod when a waiter details the steak special even though I don't eat meat. At long last, she alighted upon the reason for my visit. On a Post-It note, she drew a graph, pitting age against biology. Her pen marked the precipitous late-thirties fertility drop-off so sharply, she drew on her own desk.

"You look okay," she said, "but you might want to consider freezing your eggs."

I promised her I would think about it, intending to drop the idea into my vast bucket of denial.

In the elevator, I received a "What are you up to?" text from my boyfriend. I had not told him about this appointment, not because he would get squeamish but because he wouldn't. My main purveyor of external pressure—the opposite sex—had temporarily, perhaps permanently, closed for business. Here was a man who was open with his emotions, receptive to mine, and initiated casual discussions about the future. It was extremely disorienting. I wasn't sure I knew how to have an opinion about this without blaming everyone else for making me have it.

"At doctor's appt," I texted.

"Because you're totally knocked up?" he wrote back.

I smacked straight into the elevator doors before they had opened, like a bird who hasn't figured out how to get out of its cage.

* * *

In addition to being a questionably necessary procedure—contrary to popular belief, one's uterus does not spontaneously turn into a bag of stale tortilla chips at age forty—freezing your eggs costs a fortune. The cost is so high, I hesitate to state it here because I have worked hard to suppress the pain. You can easily find out for yourself by reading one of the many articles I refused to read. The best way I can describe the financial impact is this: I had a friend in college who had two hundred CDs stolen from his dorm room during our freshman year. He had learned to accept this loss but each time he heard a song he'd forgotten he once owned, he'd crumble into a depressed lump. For years, he basically couldn't go anywhere music might be played. This is exactly how I feel about the egg-freezing bill.

What egg freezing does is give you the illusion of a plan. An expensive illusion. I've paid far less to eat mushrooms and stare at a bedspread for an hour. But the women with the resources to pony up the cash are buying themselves time, which is, arguably, the most valuable commodity on the planet. Waylaying the inevitable doesn't come cheap. For me, time was the side dish. The entrée was brain space, the ability to release the pressure of making a decision that would impact the rest of my life and, potentially, the life of an additional human. When I looked at it this way, it almost seemed like a bargain.

Before you embark on the egg-freezing process, you have to take a class. The class is mandatory but you have to pay for it, which is a bit of a boondoggle. We arrived in the order of what kind of parent we would be. Women who got there early and sat up front would be the kind of moms who put notes in their children's lunch boxes. Women who sat in the second row would remember it was Purple Shirt Day the night before and do a stealth load of laundry. Women who sat in the back would let their kids drink in the basement. I consoled myself that at least I was not the very last person to arrive. I was the second to last. But then I had to borrow a pen from my neighbor, which set me back.

We were each given flesh-colored cushions reminiscent of ergonomic mouse pads. We had to practice pinching them as if they were our own skin, and injecting them with empty vials of medication. All the cushions were Caucasian. I don't know the exact statistics regarding the racial profile of women who get their eggs frozen but I can guess. I suppose there's an argument to be made, albeit a weak one, that it's easier for beginners to practice on something pale, to see the contrast of the needle on a mound of white-girl pseudo-flesh. But since such a creature does not exist in nature, I don't see the harm in manufacturing them all in violet or mint green.

The women in my class were advanced fertility chess players. I couldn't understand how they knew so much already. They were eight moves ahead, their hands flying skyward as they asked questions about dosages and hormone levels and how soon they could pop their frozen eggs back from whence they came. One lady asked if it was okay to have sex during the process, which is just showing off. Overwhelmed by the naked want they all shared, I stress-pinched my flesh wad. My heart raced from peer pressure. In the weeks to come, as I laid out needles like a mad scientist, consulting YouTube videos for each injection, experiencing foul moods that dripped down to my heart like black syrup, I would amuse myself by saying, "The real bitch of this whole thing is that they made us take that fucking class."

The only useful tidbit I learned is that the female reproductive system is just as dog-eat-dog as a man's. Every month, all the eggs vie to be the power egg. This queen-bee egg forces the other eggs to sulk in the corner, presumably with such bad self-esteem issues you wouldn't want one of them as your kid anyway. I had no idea that eggs were competitive like sperm. This is something we should toss into middle school health curriculums, if only for the sociological implications. My entire life, I have assumed that eggs were passive creatures, inert trophies to be earned by ambitious sperm. I blame Woody Allen.

The first step in egg freezing is to hormonally democratize this dictatorship. You inject vials of drugs into your abdomen to persuade that one egg to let everyone have a chance. At the end of two weeks, you are briefly knocked out while your eggs are popped in a freezer. And that's that . . . with one tiny snag. Whatever symptoms of PMS a woman has when she normally gets her period exist in proportion to that one egg. One egg's worth of headaches. One egg's worth of bloating. One egg's worth of wondering why everyone in your life is such a goddamn disappointment.

The average egg-freezing cycle produces between eight and fifteen eggs.

You do the math.

* * *

But first, the drugs.

The hormones alone can cost up to two thousand dollars. When I unleashed this information on my therapist, she told me she had another patient who had just undergone the process and had leftover medication. I was delighted. Especially given how much therapy costs. I had always assumed that if I bought mass quantities of drugs on the black market, they would be recreational in nature, but here we were. My therapist—our therapist—introduced us over e-mail and we arranged a time for me to come pick up the stuff.

The woman was an Indian lawyer who lived in an apartment in Chelsea, a large doormanned co-op with aggressive lobby art and confounding elevator buttons. The interior of her apartment could only be described as palatial. No wonder she was giving away drugs like candy. When I stepped inside, I was asked to remove my shoes and handed a pair of "guest slippers." In my house, I only have "guest hotel shampoos." She had changed into leggings and a T-shirt after a long day of deploying her expensive education. We stood on either side of her kitchen island.

"So, how long have you lived here?" I asked.

"About three years," she said. "I know it doesn't look like it."

"No, no," I said, "it definitely looks like it."

Visible through her open bedroom door was a large flat-screen television. *The Bachelor* was on.

"I moved in after my divorce."

"Oh," I said. "Cool."

It's hard enough to make small talk with a stranger without knowing you have the same therapist. There's a subtle jockeying for sanest. What you're both really thinking is: What are you in for?

"So you need three boxes of the Menopur and two of the Follistim, right?"

The top half of her body was obscured by the open refrigerator door as she stood on her tippy-toes.

"Yes," I said. "Thank you so much."

"You're aware that I'm selling these, right?"

"No," I said, "I was not aware of that."

"It's at least a thousand dollars' worth of medication." She stated the facts.

"That's why I was so grateful," I said, trying to laugh it off. "This is awkward."

"I couldn't figure out why you were being so nice about it," she mused.

"Nice" didn't begin to describe it. In our e-mails, I had referred to her as a "lifesaver" and a "saint." I told her she was "doing her good deed for the year." I was in for a financially and physically arduous ride, and the idea that a stranger with a heart of platinum would be so generous had renewed my faith in the capacity of women to support each other.

Later that evening, I went back and examined our correspondence. Sure enough, she had clearly listed prices next to the name of each medication. The numbers were unmistakable. The issue was, she had left the dollar signs off. That's how many boxes of drugs there are—it takes real time to type the dollar signs. Because I had never done this before, I assumed all those numbers were milligrams or micrograms or marbles. But the e-mails were not the point. Why would I assume a total stranger would part with such expensive items for free?

I wanted so badly to find just one loophole of ease, my subconscious made it so. I immediately began making justifications to myself about how I was right and she was wrong. She had found something incongruous about my appreciation and had ample opportunities to clarify the situation before I was standing in her kitchen. Not to mention the fact that these drugs had been in her possession for almost a year and would expire in a month, which meant she needed to find a buyer pronto. Selling them online would be illegal. If I knew that, she definitely knew that. Would she rather consign them to the dumpster or donate them to a clinic than give them to me? Absolutely she would.

I explained that if I was going to pay full price for nearly expired drugs, I might as well just be an upstanding citizen about it and go through a pharmacy.

"Well," she said and shrugged. "Good luck with it."

No negotiation. Case closed. She wasn't doing it to be spiteful. She wasn't even annoyed, as I surely would have been if the slipper were on the other foot. She was doing it because it was time to draw a line in the sand. She had gone through two rounds of egg freezing with negligible results. Her husband had left her for a younger woman. She was forty-four, spent her days thinking about fairness on behalf of other people, and she felt owed. And she was owed. Just as every woman who smiles through a lifetime of complicated biology and double standards is owed. But tonight, I was going to be the one to pay her.

On the television in the bedroom, a tearful girl told the camera how much she regretted "putting herself out there." I wondered if I should tell my therapist about this incident or if this woman would beat me to it.

* * *

Only the Upper West Side, a neighborhood that caters to the yet-to-be-born and the on-their-way-out, would be host to a pharmacy that specializes in both fertility meds and compression socks. I stood in line, eyeing bars of Reagan-era soap and a stunning variety of pastel candies. I tried to imagine the woman who had spent the past nine decades figuring out exactly which flavor of pastel candy she liked the best. When it was my turn, I relinquished my credit card to a cashier, who had to pry it from my fingers. As money had apparently ceased to have any meaning, I selected a couple of overpriced hair clips while he filled a supermarket bag. A few customers cast sympathetic looks in my direction. What would have to be so wrong with you that you'd walk away from a prescription counter with a shopping bag full of drugs?

"You want me to throw an ice pack in there?" asked the cashier.

"Why not?" I said. "Go crazy."

None of the medication required refrigeration unless you were going to store it for an extended time, and so long as you didn't do anything brilliant like rest it on a radiator. But at this juncture, I would take anything I didn't have to pay for. *Do you want me to throw a patty of petrified horse shit in there? Sure, why not? You only live once.*

I went straight home, put the bag on my kitchen counter, tossed the ice pack in the freezer, and threw on a dress. It was New Year's Eve. I was putting the "new year, new you" diets to shame. I would start the year as a grown-up card-carrying member of my gender, as someone who makes proactive health decisions and cowers before the reality of the future, as woman-shaped flesh wad.

The next day, I decided to familiarize myself with the drugs. I stood in my kitchen across from the bag, staring at it. But when I got up the nerve to peer inside, there were no drugs. Just the syringes, the needles and a portable toxic waste container for disposing of them. I touched the bottom of the paper, thinking vaguely of trapdoors. I could feel the anger spread across my skin. The cashier had forgotten to put my entire order of medication in the bag. Naturally, such a thing had never happened with a five-dollar prescription but of course it had with the fifteen-hundred-dollar one.

I had all of New Year's Day to stew and pace. I called when the pharmacy opened the following day, displaying a kind of barely contained rage for which I expected to be rewarded. Anything short of murder warranted a gold star. But their records showed I had picked up the medication. I explained the difference between paying for something and leaving with it. I was not trying to swindle them. I don't need the extra needles for my side gig as a methadone addict. I barely wanted these needles. I threatened to take pictures of the empty bag. Still, they maintained the drugs were in there.

"There's nothing here," I said. "There was only an ice pack and I put it in—"

There are moments in life when one literally stops in one's tracks. Usually you have to see a wild animal or a celebrity you thought was dead.

"Will you please hold?"

I opened my freezer and removed the foil pack. For the first time, I noticed a seam at the top. I ripped it open. Inside was a packet of ice the size of a playing card and boxes of medication stickered with the words HUMAN HORMONE. DO NOT FREEZE.

The reality of what I had done took no time to sink in. I, who only four nights prior had registered the wasted cab fare to Chelsea, had just destroyed fifteen hundred dollars' worth of medication by tossing it into the freezer like a bag of peas.

One wonders what I would do with an actual child.

The pharmacy had neglected to sticker the foil pouch itself and kindly agreed to send me new drugs. My case was easy to make. Improperly labeling medication is not an offense I came up with. Still, how could *two* of these misunderstandings have occurred in forty-eight hours? Has anyone's ambivalence ever run so deep? Before we hung up, I asked the pharmacist how many functioning adults had ever done what I did. He pretended to scan his memory. The answer was none. I was the "hot coffee" case of the reproductive-medicine world. Next time you think to yourself, "What kind of idiot doesn't understand that coffee is hot?" know that the answer is: This kind.

* * *

In order to freeze your eggs, you must give yourself two different types of shots, one in the morning and one in the evening, always within an hour of the time you gave yourself the first shot. This is as elaborate as it sounds. Especially compared with every other medication I'd ever taken, for which I needed only a working esophagus. My boyfriend offered to do the injections for me.

"It'll be a good bonding experience," he said, afflicted as he is with a fondness for the bright side.

"It's not like I have to take them in the ass," I reasoned.

"I'm not even touching that rationale," he said and backed off.

Some of the shots burn, others bruise, all of them force you to abandon your squeamishness around needles. The margin of error is significant. One day I didn't mix in all the saline. Another day I managed to go through all the steps and somehow wound up with an unused needle, which is a bit like winding up with extra IKEA dresser parts, but slightly worse because you're injecting the dresser into your body. Another day I sliced my finger open removing the sheath from a mixing needle. It was such a precise cut, it took a second to get comfortable with its existence before bleeding all over the place. Freezing your eggs is essentially a cheap way to become a registered nurse. But by the time you know what you're doing, you don't need to do it anymore.

Meanwhile, I went into the fertility center every day to get reacquainted with the wand. One morning, as I lay back and put my feet in the stirrups, I announced that it was the darnedest thing—the hormones were having zero effect on me. No tears, no mood swings, no irrational behavior. Finally, I was excelling at something. Then the doctor on duty turned off the lights as I was in the middle of reading from a list of questions. I cleared my throat.

"Can you just ask me during the exam?"

Perhaps I have mentioned that the exam entails a wand being shoved into your body. Not the ideal time for a Q&A.

"But you turned the lights out."

"Don't you have them memorized?" she asked.

"No," I said, feeling my voice crack. "That's why I wrote them down."

I started crying. Hysterically. Inconsolably. People outside the door probably thought I'd lost a whole baby. The doctor removed the wand and flicked the lights back on.

"It's the hormones."

I sat up. I shook my head but was too busy sobbing to speak. It was, most definitely, not the hormones. The Venn diagram of financial, psychological, and physical strain was more of a total eclipse. What's worse, I had subjected myself to all this voluntarily. I had reasons to cry. My problem was that, once triggered, I couldn't seem to get it under control. And for argument's sake, let's say it was the hormones. It seemed borderline dangerous to point it out. Try asking a pregnant woman if she's in a bad mood because of the hormones and see what happens.

* * *

My boyfriend was out of town but offered to come back early for the procedure. As a longtime mostly single person, I appreciated this relationship perk. This was right up there with going to the bathroom at the airport without having to drag your luggage into the stall with you. That and the general reprieve from being viewed by society as either threatening or pitiable. But I discouraged him. It's fifteen minutes, I explained. A power nap. People go back to work afterward. I did, however, inform my parents that I was going under anesthesia. Which meant I had to tell them why.

"I told you so," said my mother. "You *do* have a uterus!"

I asked my friend Sara to retrieve me. Hospitals won't let you walk out the door by yourself, which really makes you wonder if they're fixing people in there. Before I went under, I asked the anesthesiologist what would happen if I didn't fall asleep. Most people, she said, wondered what would happen if they never woke up. I told her this seemed like a nonsense question. Who cares? You'll be dead. Your concerns are minimal.

Again, one wonders how I would speak to an actual child.

I don't remember waking up from the procedure—"harvesting," if you'd like to lose your lunch—but apparently I was less than pleasant. When Sara tried to force-feed me a saltine, I told her to "eat it." From a padded chair, I watched other women sign their discharge papers and go, flying away to their lives. Eventually, a doctor came over and pulled a chair up next to mine. I lolled my head in her direction, waiting for her to do something insidious like ask me to take a sip of apple juice.

The doctor was younger than I was. Triangular pink diamonds swayed from her earlobes. Definitely a gift, but from whom? She was young enough for the answer to be "Daddy." As she scooted forward, the concern on her face came into focus. She looked like the kind of lady who might refuse to operate on her son.

I *knew* it, I thought. I knew that my body would not behave as it should, that all my inklings about not being a real woman had been correct.

"Something a bit unusual happened during the procedure," said the doctor.

Unusual? I rolled the word around the padded walls of my brain. Like they had to give me more drugs than expected "unusual" or they staged a revival of *Gypsy* over my unconscious body "unusual"?

Evidently, my eggs were fine, now crowded cozily together in a petri dish. But at sixty-seven, the club was at capacity.

"What?!"

I was awake now. I looked at Sara to make sure she had heard the same thing. Sixty-seven is not within the range of numbers listed in pamphlets. It's a gaudy amount of eggs for a human to produce. On some core level, I was thrilled. To go through all this and get three eggs is like reading all of *Ulysses* only to discover the last page has been ripped out. But I was also disturbed. I felt disconnected from my body, as if it had been trying to tell me something for years and I hadn't been listening. Or I had been listening but had heard the wrong thing. Because I was right. I am not a woman—I am a fish.

Sara promptly told me that I had "ruined caviar" for her.

"How often are you sitting around, eating caviar?"

"Often enough."

How, I wondered, had the daily wand molestings failed to see this coming?

"Because they were so packed in," explained the doctor, cupping her hands to approximate the shape of an egg, "like a vending machine."

"Gross," Sara and I said in unison.

* * *

One of the benefits of having gone through something so specific is the ability to rehash the details with other people who have gone through that same specific thing. We may be done with our subcutaneous injections but our subcutaneous injections are not done with us. But I learned quickly to keep my mouth shut about my egg number. If it came up, I changed the subject or indicated that the procedure had gone fine. It's a pass/fail world and I passed. Number disclosure is considered as gauche as bragging about your massive pay increase for doing the exact same job as your coworker. Many women find it insensitive. It's how I feel about straight-haired beauties who get a thrill out of humidity. Know your audience, I think, tallying up a lifetime of hair products, keeping my hands in my pockets so I don't throttle these shaggy-banged bitches. Seeing as how we're dealing with the potential for human life, the throttling urge is that much stronger.

To so badly want a baby and not be able to have one is a peerless brand of devastating. Everyone knows this. Fictionally, it turns women deranged (*The Hand That Rocks the Cradle*) and men monstrous (*The Handmaid's Tale*). In real life, it just makes everybody sad. I am not in the habit of making people feel bad about themselves when they can do that on their own. And if it were just about hurt feelings, I'd continue to stay mum. I wouldn't even have revealed my number here. But there was something rotten in the state of Denmark.

By freezing my eggs, I had stuck my toe into the world of competitive female biology. Women who had plenty of eggs retrieved (but still within the realm of reason) confessed something like pride in their number. They flaunted their results under the guise of relief. I want to distinguish myself from them. I was not so lucky as I looked, I explained. My big payout had come at a high cost. Mo' eggs, mo' problems. After the procedure, I was treated to a panoply of medical complications including a *Tales from the Crypt*–style syndrome in which one's abdominal region retains multiple liters of water in ten hours. For me, this also resulted in a bonus surgery. Boy, had I been through the wringer!

I listened to myself recite all this, trying to fend off judgment. Was it really necessary for me to drag out stories of additional specialists in order to justify telling the truth? *I won the lottery but my dog exploded, so, you know.*

But even the complications couldn't get me out of jail. When

I told a friend who'd always been dyspeptic about having kids, she was unable to hide her disgust.

"See?" she said, assured of her own choices. "This is why it's not worth it."

Which is a bit like critiquing someone's e-mail to their ex after they've sent it.

When I told one mother of three, she replied with: "Well, now you know what it feels like to be pregnant." Not quite. Being pregnant is a natural occurrence. You don't become six months pregnant over ten excruciating hours. It is my understanding that you also get a baby out of it. Now whose turn was it to be offended?

This was getting ugly.

The thing is, even if I had produced two eggs, I like to believe I would have been forthright about it. It's impossible to say. But I know for certain that focusing on the math as the defining moment of one's life only perpetuates the idea of fertility as identity. This isn't the seventeenth century. Nor is it the dystopian future. There doesn't have to be social meaning. There only has to be personal meaning. Tell everyone, tell no one. Read the articles, don't read the articles, find kinship or alienation in them, it doesn't matter. By virtue of them being written by someone else, none of them are prescribed for you and you alone. When it comes to your own life, there is only one location in the world where the right decisions are being kept. Which, come to think of it, is the kind of thing I would tell an actual child.

* * *

The children are coming, the children are coming. I would have sent that intuitor his tip if I hadn't just broken the bank proving him right. My transcendental Paul Revere had succeeded where a magic wand had failed. But his prophecy felt less ominous now. The children are en route, okay, but they could always change their minds. My eggs are frozen in a cryobank in Midtown—they don't have any travel plans. For months after the procedure, I would get automated updates from the cryobank using language that made me feel as if I'd arranged to freeze my head.

Then one day I was walking up my apartment stairs, flipping through junk mail, when I came across an envelope with the cryobank's logo. My eggs had never sent me actual mail before. *Camp is fun. We are cold.* The letter explained that enclosed was "a representative photomicrograph of your oocytes frozen during the cryopreservation cycle." I mean, they really go out of their way to make it sound like you're freezing your head. I moved the letter aside to reveal a piece of paper with a black-and-white photograph of my eggs. They looked like the marks that would appear if you pressed a pen cap into your skin sixty-seven times. Or craters on the surface of some very distant moon.

They are just floating fractions of an idea. I know that. But I had never seen a part of my body exist outside my body before. I felt such gratitude. My eggs had held up their end of the bargain. They had saved me from having to think about them, which, for the first time in my life, made me want to think about them. This doesn't mean I know what will become of them. Maybe I have a baby. Maybe none. Maybe eight. Maybe I sell them all on the black market, buy a townhouse and forget this whole thing ever happened. But sometimes when I'm alone, I run my fingers over the photo, even though it doesn't feel like anything. I focus on one egg at random, imagining this will be the one my body uses to make a person, a person that grows up and reads this, and I think—Oh girl, I hope you set the world on fire.

Acknowledgments

Thanks to Jay Mandel, Sean McDonald, Jonathan Galassi, Jeff Seroy, Kimberly Burns, Sarah Scire, and everyone at FSG. And to my friends and family, whose love is a steady reminder that this life is the very best one I'll ever have.